The World's Longest Taxi Fare

Geelong to Darwin and return in Charlie Heard's Hudson

Larry O'Toole

Published in 2014 by Graffiti Publications Pty. Ltd.,
69 Forest Street, Castlemaine, Victoria, Australia
Phone International 61 3 5472 3653 Email: info@graffitipub.com.au
www.graffitipub.com.au
Copyright © 2014 by Larry O'Toole
Publisher: Larry O'Toole
Design: Michael Wolfe

Graffiti Publications books are also available at discounts in bulk quantity for industrial
or sales promotional use. For details contact Graffiti Publications Ph: (613) 5472 3653
Printed in China by SC (Sang Choy) International Pte Ltd.

National Library of Australia Cataloguing-in-Publication entry
Author: O'Toole, Larry, author.
Title: The world's longest taxi fare : Geelong to Darwin and return
            in Charlie Heard's Hudson / Larry O'Toole.
ISBN: 9780949398990 (hardback)
Notes: Includes bibliographical references.
Subjects: Heard, Charlie--Journeys--Australia.
            Taxicab drivers--Australia--Anecdotes.
            Taxicabs--Australia--Anecdotes.
            Australia--Description and travel.
Dewey Number: 388.4132140994

■ Contents

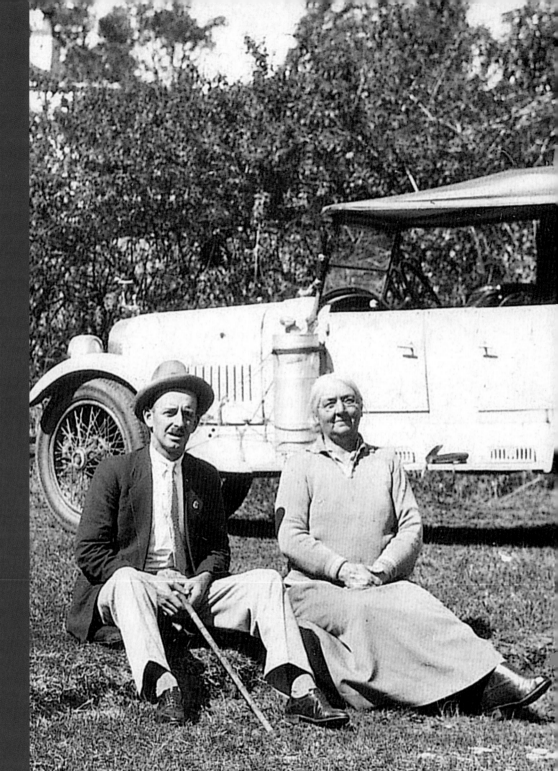

■ Introduction

Before the Second World War, recreational travel through the outback

and central Australia was rarely undertaken. Motor vehicles were still somewhat of a luxury item and there were few made roads once you were clear of the major population centres. Prior to the 1920s almost all freight was carried inland by bullock wagons, horse teams or camel trains. Very few people made motor car trips that weren't absolutely necessary, as there was little in the way of services available anywhere in the outback. The first motorists who traversed the centre of Australia had to rely on petrol supplies that were transported to where they would be needed by rail, as far as they extended, and then by camel trains deep into the interior.

That's how it was for Motor Service Provider Charlie Heard, when he was engaged to carry three ladies on a daring adventure from Lorne in Victoria, up through the red centre to Darwin and back down to Melbourne via Brisbane and Sydney. The world's longest taxi fare was a journey of incredible proportions, considering it took place in 1930, as the world was heading into the great depression. Many areas of the outback were only just beginning to be properly explored and mapped, and made roads were still almost non-existent.

Ada Beal was an adventurous spinster from western Victoria, who had inherited some wealth and even though she had an artificial leg, and was aged 66 years, she decided an adventure to the outback was something that women of her era should be prepared to undertake. It was she who engaged Charlie Heard to provide the transport for this epic trip. Ada paid for everything, from camping equipment to alterations to Charlie's Hudson car to make it suitable to undertake the trip. She paid Charlie his normal taxi rate, all fuel and accommodation costs, and extra where the price of fuel was abnormally high.

Ada Beal's fellow travellers were Eileen Glenny, from Ballarat and Lil Wilmot from Melbourne. Eileen was much younger than Ada and Lil, and it appears she may have been Ada Beal's personal assistant for the trip.

In order to gain a clear perspective of how significant this expedition was at the time, it is necessary to explore a little of the history of the outback areas where they travelled. While the coastal fringes of Australia were well settled by the middle of the nineteenth century, inland exploration and expansion was a much slower process.

Unsuccessful attempts at crossing the centre from south to north were made by Edward John Eyre in 1840 and Charles Sturt in 1844. Eyre was stopped by what he thought was a large salt lake extending from east to west. In fact, it was later realised, there were several separate lakes extending through this area including Lake Gairdner, Lake Torrens and Lake Frome.

John McDouall Stuart was a member of Sturt's unsuccessful 1844 expedition party. He set out on his own expedition on March 2, 1860 and reached as far as Attack Creek, north of present day Tennant Creek, where hostile natives and lack of stores forced him back to Adelaide. In November 1861 he tried again, only making it about 100 miles further north, where impenetrable forest and scrub thwarted him once more. A third attempt was made from Adelaide on October 26, 1861 and this time he made it through, striking the coast to the east of Adelaide River on July 24, 1862. He almost perished on the return journey, but eventually made it back to Adelaide.

Burke and Wills attempted the same feat from Melbourne to the Gulf of Carpentaria in August 1860, but that attempt ended in the well documented disaster where only King survived from the small party that struck out from Cooper Creek in a rush to be the first to make the crossing from south to north.

The Overland Telegraph line was commissioned in 1870 when John Ross followed Stuart's track, for the most part, surveying the route for the line from Adelaide to Darwin. He was the first white man to reach Central Australia after Stuart. Charles Todd, the Post Master General, Superintendent of Telegraphs and the Government Astronomer of South Australia was responsible for building the line that was planned to take place over a period of 18 months. In fact it took 25 months, still an incredible achievement, considering the distance covered and the conditions encountered by the construction crews. It was Charles Todd who commissioned John Ross to make the survey of the proposed route. Ross named the Todd River after his boss. Ross was a good bushman and explorer and was resourceful in overcoming problems.

The first northern pole was placed at Port Darwin on September 15, 1870, while the first southern pole was put in place on October 1, 1870. The telegraph line was joined at Frew's Pond, south of Daly Waters on July 22, 1872. Originally all the poles were wooden but they were quickly eaten by termites and replaced with wrought iron "Oppenheimer poles" that could be telescoped down for transport by camel trains. Once completed the Overland Telegraph Line became the established route for travellers heading north and south through the centre. EM Bagot was the successful tenderer for the southern section of the Overland Telegraph Line from Port Augusta 500 miles to the north and this section was known as "Bagot's Line".

Jerome Murif became the first person to cross from Adelaide to Darwin by bicycle in 1897, taking 74 days to complete the journey with a rest period at Alice Springs on the way through. Albert MacDonald rode his bicycle from Darwin to Melbourne in a short 33 days in 1898, averaging 125 kilometres per day.

Francis Birtles was prolific in crossing the continent. In fact he had crossed it seven times and ridden around it twice on his bicycle between 1905 and 1912. Then he took to motoring and made more than 70 trips prior to 1928, when he became the first person to drive from London to Melbourne.

A lone walker turned up at Alice Springs Overland Telegraph Station early in the 1900s having walked from Gawler, 25 miles north of Adelaide. He continued on alone to Darwin after resting for a few days, stayed in Darwin for three months working, then walked back to Adelaide, claiming he didn't like Darwin.

Stock routes criss-crossed the inland, some following at least parts of the Overland Telegraph Line. Water bores were established along the Telegraph Line route and later private bores were added across the Barkly Tableland by 1914. In 1917 another 13 bores, (25 miles apart) were added by the Government. Overland travellers and mail coaches naturally followed the same routes, but the water wasn't always good.

The railway commenced from Port Augusta in 1876 and followed a route through Quorn, Beltana (opened 1881) and then on to Oodnadatta where it terminated in 1891. For 30 years Oodnadatta remained the railhead and camel trains were still used from there to the north. The rail extension to Alice Springs was commenced on January 21, 1927 and was opened through to Alice Springs in 1929, the first train reaching there on August 6, 1929. Later still the route of the railway line was changed, no longer passing through Marree (formerly Hergott Springs) and Oodnadatta, but following the east-west route from Port Augusta to Tarcoola, where it turns north to Alice Springs, passing just to the west of Coober Pedy.

From Darwin, a southern rail line commenced in August 1886 and the first train left on July 16, 1888. The line reached Pine Creek in October 1889, after 300 bridges and flood crossings were built, necessary to allow it to operate in the wet season. The line was later extended to Katherine and then on to Birdum (also known as No. 2 Bore) where it terminated. Only in January, 2004 was the connection made between the south and north rail lines, making a rail trip possible between Adelaide and Darwin.

The Northern Australia Act came into being in 1926, creating the new territory of Central Australia. In 1929 Alice Springs opened a new Police Station with three resident policemen. Although the Telegraph Station was at Alice Springs the nearby township was only named such in 1933, formerly being referred to as Stuart. Alice Springs was named after Charles Todd's wife.

Motor car trips north and south

Henry Dutton and Murray Aunger tried to cross from south to north in 1907 in a 24 HP Talbot when no car had been further north than Hawker. They reached Alice Springs in December, after some difficulty, and had to abandon the car south of Tennant Creek, when it became stuck in an impassable bog. They tried again in 1908 with a 25 HP Talbot. Ernest Allchurch, the Postmaster at Alice Springs at the time, joined them on this trip and they left Adelaide on June 30. They reached the other Talbot before the end of July and found it untouched, despite being left there for eight

Dutton and Aunger set off in their 24 HP Talbot on the first attempt to cross from Adelaide to Darwin in 1907.

The route followed by Dutton and Aunger in 1907/08 followed the telegraph line for much of the way. Note the reference to where the first car was abandoned in 1907.

months. It was repaired and the party continued with both cars. The first Talbot was put on the train at Pine Creek and the other was driven to Darwin, arriving on August 20, 1908.

In 1922 Murray Aunger was again involved in a south to north crossing, this time using three Dort cars, supplied by his and brother Cyril's Adelaide based garage and travelling via Oodnadatta. Aunger and Captain SA White drove these fenderless and doorless Dort cars to Darwin and back, leaving Adelaide in May 1922.

Thomas McCallum, the politician and local statesman of the Coorong district had spoken to White about a trip across Australia from south to north and back again. The trip was to ascertain the suitability of running the north-south railway from Adelaide to Darwin and to gauge the value of the land they traversed and the feelings of the people who lived there. McCallum and his brother Donald were to advise the Government on the possibilities of further settlement along the route they travelled. The McCallums financed the expedition and Mr H Crowder was the other member of the party. The arranging of stores for the trip was particularly arduous as they had to be available at points along the route from Adelaide to Darwin.

News of the journey spread throughout the world with many of White's scientific contemporaries expressing envy at being able to undertake such a trip. The expedition left Adelaide on May 9, 1922, to great cheering from the large crowd that gathered at the GPO. When they reached Wilmington a local inhabitant prophesied that; "They will

First to attempt to cross the continent from south to north by motor vehicle were Henry Dutton and Murray Aunger in 1907, driving a 24 HP Talbot. They had to abandon the attempt, and the car, near Tennant Creek when the track became too boggy. They returned in 1908 with a 25 HP Talbot, rescued the first car and continued to Darwin, reaching there on August 20, 1908.

To assist in climbing the soft sand dunes, typically found in the Depot Hills, Stepney wheels were attached to the normal wheels to gain better traction. The rolls of coir matting on the rear were also rolled out to allow the vehicle to maintain traction while climbing up sand dunes.

Murray Aunger performed an incredible feat by driving a Dort car through a flooded creek north of Newcastle Waters that was so deep only his upper torso and the steering wheel of the car was visible above the water. He made it to the other side.

get as far as Horseshoe Bend, and that will finish them". It didn't and they reached Alice Springs on May 17 at 7:00pm. The party left again on May 21 after Donald McCallum recovered from an illness. By May 23 they had reached Barrow Creek telegraph station where they stayed for another two days. They left again on May 25 only to catch up with a camel train carrying their stores only 40 kilometres further on. These stores were supposed to be 160 kilometres ahead of them at this stage. There was no option but to load everything onto the cars and continue. More trouble came when the lead car suffered overheating from grass seeds clogging the radiator.

Tennant Creek was reached on May 27 and described as a desolate spot. North of Newcastle Waters they encountered a broad, swift flowing creek. A local Aborigine tested the depth for them and described it as; "flurry deep". It was actually about 2.5 metres deep but Aunger decided to try taking a car across. He stood on the seat and gripped the steering wheel as he entered the water. As the front of the car was submerged, great bubbles arose from the tortured engine. Aunger felt the water gradually creep up his body until only part of his shoulders, his neck and his head were above it. White perched himself on a tree on the opposite bank to photograph this amazing escapade. One of those photos shows the feat exactly as described here, in the book "Nature's Pilgrim", from which much of this information has been transcribed.

The going became very rough as they came out onto the Sturt Plain where they were met by a vast sea of grass. As the expedition was travelling through the country between Daly Waters and Katherine, they came across the first gate they had encountered in 2250 kilometres. They reached Darwin on the evening of June 7, where they stayed until June 11. On the return trip their cars went on the train with them back to Pine Creek and by noon on June 13 they were all loaded up again in the cars, ready for departure from the Katherine River. By June 15 they were at Birdum Creek. Nearing Newcastle Waters again they were greeted by sheets of water that made the going very muddy and difficult, but by June 17 they were through it and back onto the fearfully rough Sturt Plain and began working along the route that followed the bores toward the Queensland border. Day after day they battled on across rough country east of Powell Creek, past Eva Downs and into

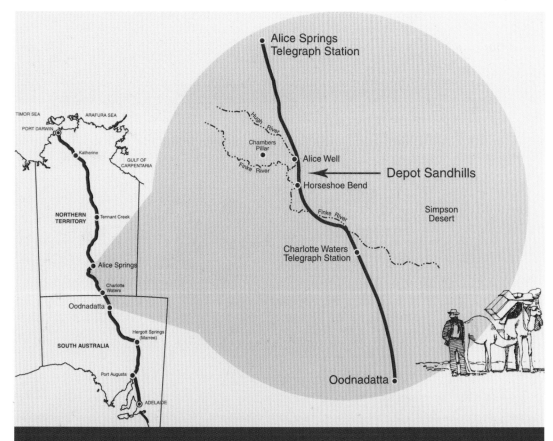

This diagram from a tourist information display in Alice Springs indicates the location of the notorious Depot Sand Hills that proved a major problem for early attempts to drive through the centre by motor vehicle.

the Barkly Tableland. After Avon Downs the country turned bleak and desolate in stark contrast to the hundreds of kilometres of dense, waving grass. On June 22 they reached Camooweal, just over the Queensland border.

From the border the expedition headed for Cloncurry and then toward Winton. After working along the Diamantina River near Barcaldine Station they were caught in a deluge that stranded them for two nights without cover and exposed to torrential rain. The damp weather began to have a negative affect on the party members, particularly Tom McCallum who went quite cranky.

Their journey didn't resume until July 1 and they were glad to get moving again. For the next fortnight they maintained a fast pace through Charleville, Cunnamulla, Barringun and Bourke where they crossed the Darling River and raced on to Wilcannia. The party forced their way through plagues of rabbits between Tolarno and Pooncarie and then moved on toward Mildura. Here there had been more very wet weather, making all of Mildura very muddy. There were arguments over which way to go next, but in the end they travelled to Ouyen, Tempy, Lascelles, Woomelang,

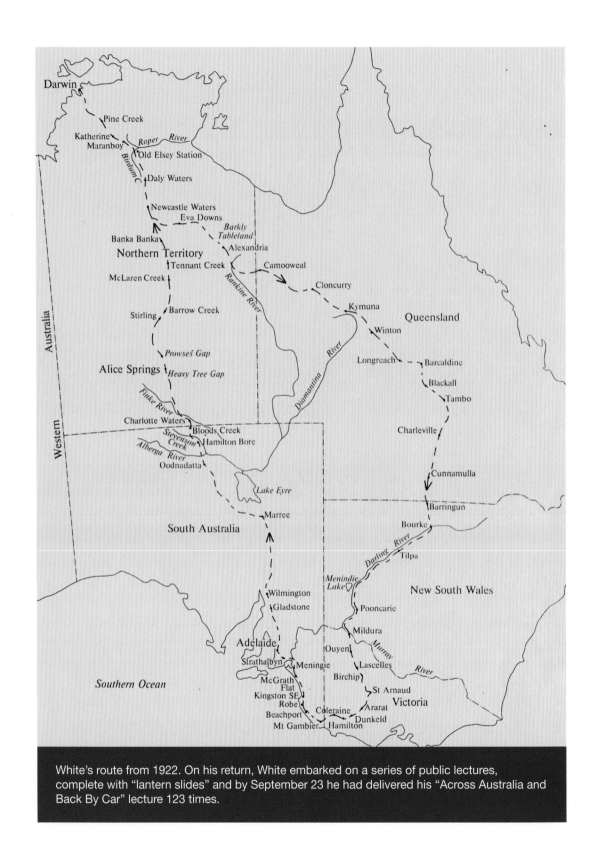

White's route from 1922. On his return, White embarked on a series of public lectures, complete with "lantern slides" and by September 23 he had delivered his "Across Australia and Back By Car" lecture 123 times.

Birchip, Watchem, Donald, St Arnaud, Ararat, Dunkeld, Hamilton, Coleraine and Mount Gambier, which they reached to a rousing reception on July 13. From Mount Gambier they proceeded along the coast past Beachport, Robe, Kingston and stopped briefly at McGrath Flat to drop off the McCallums. They reached Adelaide on July 15 where once again there was a large crowd to greet them with cheers. In 10 weeks they covered 5470 miles.

On his return, White embarked on a series of public lectures, complete with "lantern slides" and by September 23 he had delivered his "Across Australia and Back By Car" lecture 123 times.

In 1923 the SA Governor Sir Thomas Bridges arrived in Alice Springs in one of these same fenderless Dort cars driven by Mr Murray Aunger.

Eventually Shell Petroleum agencies were established through the centre of Australia, supplied by the Ghan train and the Afghan camel trains after which it was named.

Among others who made the north-south journey by motor car in the 1920s were the Earl of Stradbroke and his party in 1924, Mr Dunkerley and Mr WF Knight in a large motor lorry in 1925, and Miss McKellar and her mother from Geelong in 1926.

In 1925 Richard Ford and two friends travelled from Adelaide to Darwin in a Crossley car, following the familiar Overland Telegraph Line, staying at places like Alice Springs, Banka Banka and Powell's Creek. The journey home included Newcastle Waters, Anthony's Lagoon, Brunette Downs and across into Queensland.

Frederick Urquhart, Northern Territory Administrator from 1921 to 1926, reported in 1925 that "the main roads of the Northern Territory are in good order." Others begged to differ. Commonwealth Resident Engineer David Douglas Smith first came to the Territory in 1927 with a survey party and later recalled that when he arrived "all roads were simply bush tracks or wheel ruts."

Malcolm Ellis made the first trip from Sydney to Darwin and back in 1924 in a 14 horsepower Bean with Francis Birtles and JL Simpson, the Bean car company's representative in Australia.

By the mid-1920s group tours were starting to emerge. In 1926 Captain EDA Bagot mounted two motor trips to Darwin from Adelaide. He promised a "unique opportunity for businessmen, prospectors, tourists and those seeking an ideal holiday, of viewing territory unknown to the majority of travellers." From the railhead at Oodnadatta, the tour group headed north in a convoy consisting of "two speedy, comfortable, eight seater Studebakers and two baggage cars." The party caught the train from Katherine to Darwin where they received a civic reception and remained for a few days, before returning to the cars to motor back to Adelaide through Queensland and down the Birdsville Track. The entire journey lasted for over five weeks. The second journey took even longer as a result of mechanical problems at Banka Banka Station and on the way back along the Boulia Road. The trips were expensive and even though Bagot collected information for possible aerodrome sites along the way for the Department of Defence, and wrote detailed descriptions of the Adelaide to Darwin route, he had to abandon his plans for a regular service due to the financial difficulties resulting from the second trip.

In August 1927 the Victorian Railways, in co-operation with its Commonwealth and South Australian counterparts, organised a "Reso" group of 60 passengers and 30 officials to travel to

Central Australia. These "Reso" tours were designed to provide a means of combining tourism and business while improving railway revenue. Most participants however, were local residents, mostly from Victoria and South Australia, with pastoral, financial, manufacturing, retail and political interests. The 1927 group, that included John Flynn and naturalist Charles Barrett, left Oodnadatta to travel to Central Mount Stuart in 15 Dodge touring cars and three service vehicles, with Murray Aunger as the "Motor Captain".

This trip was one of three motor car tours of Central Australia made in 1927. AG (Bert) Bond, a bus operator from South Australia, used two Studebakers to carry a party of nine passengers from Oodnadatta to Bullion Mines, north of Barrow Creek. On the way back they camped beside the "Reso" party at Horseshoe Bend and between Anna Creek and Coober Pedy they met a coach party consisting of 11 people. They were on the first tour to the Territory organised by the Melbourne based Pioneer company. They were heading for Darwin and were to return via Longreach and Sydney. The Bond tourists also met four private motoring parties.

The following year Bond took a group of paying passengers and his wife Doreen up to Darwin. Despite tyre punctures and leaking petrol tanks, they managed to get to Katherine where they caught the train. On the way back, at Ryan's Well, the Bond group met the 1928 Pioneer tour party heading for Darwin. The outback was beginning to open up to paying tourists.

Two ladies attempted to drive around Australia in 1927, Gladys Sandford and Stella Christie. Stella didn't drive so Gladys did all of the driving on her own in a two door Essex Coach. They were forced back by floods north of Perth so they drove back across the Nullabor and then up through the centre to Katherine. The last stretch to Darwin was done with the car on the train, but they drove the return trip to Katherine in the car, taking five days to make the journey.

Aircraft travel was also emerging in the outback during the 1920s with Donald MacKay making an aerial survey of the western and south western portions of Central Australia in May and June 1930. The Mackay aerial expedition was established at Ilbilba, west of Alice Springs. A 54 camel train was used to transport fuel to Ilbilba for the aeroplanes.

In 1927 a Mr Muir (a dentist) is reported to have made a south to north crossing of the continent by motor car and in 1928 Hector Macquarie and Richard Matthews drove from Sydney to Cape York in a Baby Austin named "Emily 1".

The general advice to travellers heading from Adelaide to Darwin in 1929 was to go from Adelaide to Hawker, then Marree and Oodnadatta, but there was less sand encountered by going from Adelaide to Port Augusta, Kingoonya, Coober Pedy and then to Oodnadatta. This was the route taken by Charlie Heard and his lady passengers.

The first vehicle to travel from Gordon Downs in Western Australia to Coniston in Central Australia, was a Morris commercial truck driven by Michael Terry in 1928, arriving in Stuart on September 3, 1928. He also made the first motor tracks between Mount Conner and the Petermann Range, meeting up with Charlie Heard and his passengers as he was setting off to establish these routes.

Frank and Win Wright, a married couple in their early thirties, made the south to north crossing in 1929 in a 1925 23/60 Vauxhall tourer, leaving from Heidelberg in Melbourne on June 15 and

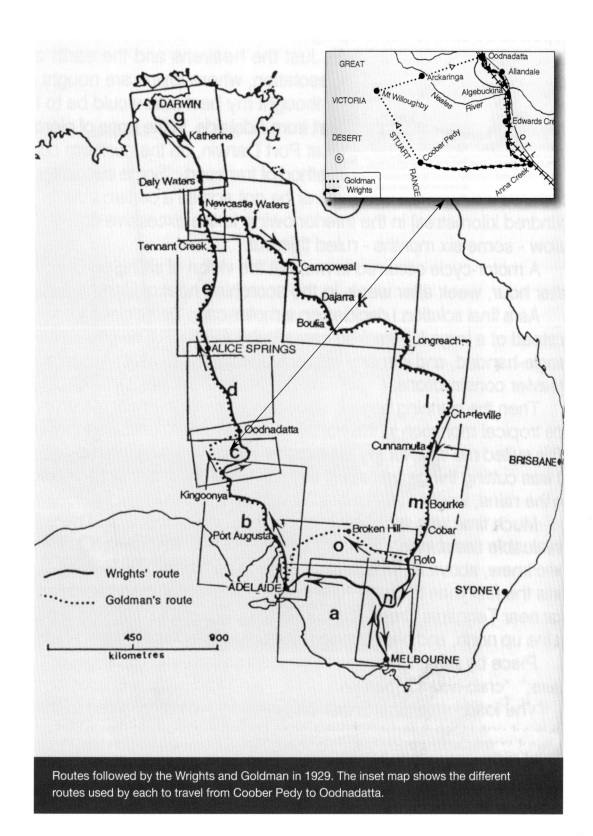

Routes followed by the Wrights and Goldman in 1929. The inset map shows the different routes used by each to travel from Coober Pedy to Oodnadatta.

travelling to Adelaide via a family property in south west NSW. They reached Darwin on July 12, stored their car and sailed to Malaysia for two months to visit Frank's sister.

Englishman Penryn Goldman, who was only 18 at the time, made the same attempt but left six weeks later on August 4 in a Baby Austin that he had to abandon at Daly Waters. He reached there the same day as the Wrights, who were on their way back south. Goldman travelled with them all the way through the Barkly Tableland, central Queensland and western NSW until they reached Roto Siding, where he caught the train back to Adelaide. Goldman received £48 for the car after it had been repaired in the Northern Territory and sold to a postal official in Darwin. Prior to their trip the Wrights had already driven a Buick car across the United States of America.

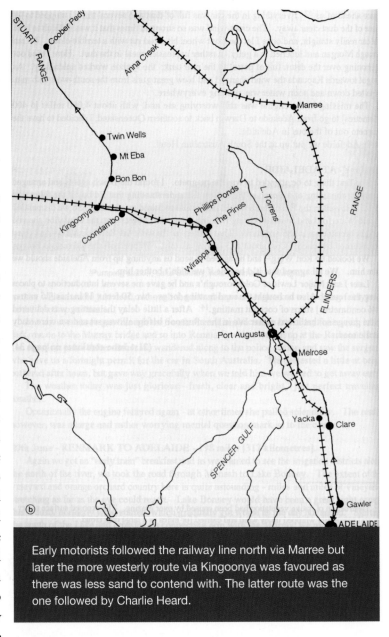

Early motorists followed the railway line north via Marree but later the more westerly route via Kingoonya was favoured as there was less sand to contend with. The latter route was the one followed by Charlie Heard.

In 1929 a big Packard travelled from Sydney via Queensland with four land seekers and a driver on board. In the same year Mr Jackson and two Wilson brothers all drove from Melbourne in a Ford ute, closely following the Wrights through the centre.

During the four years leading up to 1929 there was severe drought across most of Australia. Most inland routes were short of water and eaten bare by hungry animals. Severe dust storms were prevalent, sometimes lasting up to three days. Then in early 1930 there was torrential rain in the centre, flooding the normally dry rivers and washing away many of the bridges and crossings, making travel almost impossible. Charlie Heard and his three lady passengers were amongst the first to make it through by motor vehicle after these floods and they were the first to actually drive into Darwin after the wet season that year.

Finally, I would like to add a note about my research for

Charlie Heard's photo album lay undisturbed in his daughter's wardrobe for almost 50 years and his grandchildren didn't know of its existence until many years after his death. Many of the photos in this book were scanned from the small photos in this album.

this book. Many sources were used to gain information about the crossing of inland Australia and I have tried to include all of those sources in the acknowledgement section. Often, essentially the same information was gleaned from several different sources that I was then able to merge together for a more complete description. Wherever possible I have tried to corroborate information and maintain authenticity with established historical records.

The story of Charlie Heard's Longest Taxi Fare is essentially based on a diary kept by himself and notes from his photo album, plus oral history from his descendants. I have used many other sources to add more detail to their basic information. Some parts of the story have been slightly embellished in the interests of reader entertainment, but the core information is as accurate as possible, given that all of the participants have since passed away. Many of the photographs used in this book came from Charlie Heard's own photo album.

In the interests of autheticity and in keeping with the language if the day, imperial measurements have been retained throughout this book, with some reference to metric equivalents where considered appropriate.

Larry O'Toole

■ Chapter

1

A proposition from Ada Beal

Charlie

Heard sat in his taxi, dreaming of the day he might own his own garage. It was a quiet afternoon in late May and Charlie was next in line for a fare. The city streets of Geelong provided Charlie with his usual customers, rarely was he required to drive far from the central area. If local residents needed to travel outside the city, they would take the train. Few people owned a vehicle of their own in those days. Such luxuries were still in the realm of the more well to do in 1930, even though Henry Ford had made ownership of a car much more available to the masses with the release of his famous Model T in the first decade of the century.

Ford's influence had recently become prominent in Geelong, when Henry opened his factory there in 1927. Now many locals relied on Ford for their employment and the Geelong economy received a huge boost as a result.

But Charlie's vehicle of choice wasn't a Ford. His taxi was a much larger vehicle, a sturdy Hudson Super Six tourer with cream paintwork and a black folding top. It could handle several passengers and a fair amount of luggage. Maybe that's why it appealed to Miss Ada Beal on that late Autumn day.

While Charlie sat there dreaming of what might be, his mind wandered back to the days of his childhood in country Victoria. Born at Rochester in 1897, he had joined up for service with the AIF in the First World War at just 16 years of age. He saw action in France during that conflict, but survived and returned to Victoria to operate a billiard room and barber-shop in Numurkah after the war.

In 1919 Charlie married Hazel Conley from Nathalia and in a few short years they had started a family, moved several times and finally settled in Geelong, where they lived in a rented house on the Melbourne road. At first Charlie, like many of his fellow war veterans, was employed on the Great Ocean Road project, a scheme that was funded by the government to help assimilate soldiers back into normal life. Charlie even operated the toll-gate on the road when it first opened, but needing to care for a growing family, he was always on the lookout for something better. By 1930 Charlie Heard had saved enough to purchase a car and become a "Motor Service Provider", now known as a taxi driver. His life was about to take a dramatic new direction.

Charlie had almost dozed off when he was suddenly startled by the presence of a woman in a fur coat, standing at the passenger door of his Hudson, with her walking stick resting on the door.

"Driver," asked the lady, "Would you be interested in a long fare?"

Charlie quickly collected his thoughts, straightened up in his driver's seat and responded, "Why, yes of course," thinking this mature looking woman of evident means would probably like a ride to Melbourne, a trip of some 50 miles to the north.

"Would you be wanting to go to Melbourne?" enquired Charlie.

"What is your name?" asked Charlie's potential customer.

"Charles Heard, ma'am."

"I'm Miss Ada Beal from Lorne, Mr. Heard, my friends and I would like to go a little further than to Melbourne," she said. "We would like to make an excursion to Darwin and back! Will you accept the fare?"

Charlie swallowed hard and thought he may not have heard her clearly, but no, she definitely said Darwin, thousands of miles away at the opposite end of Australia.

"That's quite a trip," said Charlie, "One that would need a lot of resources and I couldn't possibly agree without consulting my wife. We have four young children you see."

"Well Mr. Heard, we would like to leave by the middle of June to take advantage of the best weather up north, so talk to your family and let me know if you will take the fare. I am prepared to meet all of the costs."

—

Ada Beal had already turned 66 when she approached Charlie Heard with her outback adventure. A spinster, she had inherited large properties, including farms, and was quite an adventurous lady, despite her advancing years. Quite apart from her adventurous spirit, she wanted to prove that women could successfully undertake an outback journey in a manner that would offer new surroundings and a wide variety of experiences. More than that, she wanted to share those experiences with her two close friends.

Lil Wilmott and Eileen Glenny were also spinsters who shared Ada's sense of adventure and agreed to make the trip to Darwin and return. Lil lived in Melbourne and Eileen in Ballarat, but both stayed in regular contact with Ada, planning their excursion over several months, leading up to Miss Beal's approach to Charlie Heard.

Ada Beal used a walking stick because she had an artificial leg. The ever present fur coat and the dignified attitude to such private matters were normal for the period, so it wasn't readily apparent. Charlie Heard certainly never referred to Miss Beal's handicap, even though he spent more than three months in close proximity with the three ladies.

Formality was the norm for the social life of the 1930s, when the depression was still being felt, and it remained in place on this journey to the top of Australia and back. The three ladies were always referred to as Miss Beal, Miss Wilmott and Miss Glenny and Charlie Heard was never addressed in that manner by the women, it was always "Mr. Heard".

—

"Hazel", called Charlie as he bounced through the door, "You won't believe what happened today." Battling with the constant needs of four young children meant Hazel was only partly listening to

Charlie's conversation as he began to describe his chance meeting with Miss Beal.

"Where did you say she wants to go?" asked Hazel when she realised that Charlie had mentioned Darwin. "You did say Darwin, didn't you? In the Northern Territory?"

"Yes," said Charlie, "And she has offered to cover all the expenses in addition to my normal taxi fare rates."

"But you would be away for months," added Hazel, "How will we cope while you're gone? What if the car breaks down? There aren't any roads up there. Doesn't it rain and flood a lot in Darwin?"

All of these doubts cascaded through Hazel's mind as she contemplated being without the family provider for such an extended period.

"This could be the chance of a lifetime," pleaded Charlie. "Miss Beal has offered to cover everything we need for the trip and it will certainly be the best fare I am ever likely to get with the taxi. We could clear our debts and purchase the garage I have always wanted. Besides Mervyn is nine years old now, he is old enough to be the man of the house while I am gone and it's time Vemba, Norma and Dawn learnt how to help you with the housework. We may never get another opportunity like this."

Tears welled in Hazel's eyes as she sat down to think more about what Charlie had just suggested. How would she cope with her husband gone for three or four months? But then the money would be welcome too. It would sure be a relief to clear their debts and set themselves up for the future. There was the children's future to think of too. Maybe they could afford better education for them? All of these thoughts were racing through Hazel's mind as she struggled to come to terms with this huge undertaking.

"Give me a little time to think about it," she offered, "I can't think straight right now, it's all a bit much."

"But Miss Beal wants an answer as soon as possible," said Charlie, "She wants to leave by the middle of June so that we get to Darwin before the weather turns hot again. Besides the wet season is finishing now, so this is the best time to go."

"Let me sleep on it," Hazel responded, "Maybe I will be able to think more clearly by tomorrow morning."

Charlie and Hazel put the children to bed a little earlier that night, they needed some extra time together to talk about this unusual request. Long into the night they talked and talked about the expedition to Darwin, Charlie ever keen to take it on, Hazel seeing the opportunity, but cautious at the same time.

Wide awake in their beds, the children listened to the murmur of their parents voices in the kitchen. Every so often they would catch just a few words, sometimes mum would cry a little, other times they would hear the excited tones of dad's eagerness for the trip. Eventually the children nodded off to sleep, the earnest discussion still filtering through to their bedrooms, but their tired eyes no longer able to stay open. Something unusual was happening, that was for sure.

—

"Miss Beal," Charlie was almost shouting into the public telephone outside the Geelong Post Office, "My wife and I have agreed to accept your proposal. The trip to Darwin can go ahead, but I need some time to get the Hudson ready."

"Well thank you, Mr Heard," was the considered response from Miss Beal, "I will travel up to Geelong tomorrow and we can discuss the requirements for the trip in detail."

Ada Beal went about her daily ritual at "Llandoo" her neatly appointed home in Lorne, but she would often catch herself dreaming about the trek she was about to make with Lil and Eileen in that nice Mr Heard's Hudson taxi. He seemed a capable fellow, probably a result of a country upbringing, but there were still some niggling doubts.

"I hope I have made the right choice," she thought to herself, "but I must stay positive, we have decided we are going to do this trip and we are jolly well going to make it work."

Miss Beal spent the rest of that day jotting down things they would need for the trip. She would need a list for Mr. Heard in the morning, better not forget anything as there were only a couple of weeks to get everything ready.

Chapter

2

Preparing for the Expedition

Providence played a big hand when Ada Beal

approached Charlie Heard to ask if he would take her little group on the world's longest taxi ride. She could hardly have chosen a more capable driver. Miss Beal suggested that Charlie should take his Hudson to a nominated coach-builder and have it checked and modified for the trip. In truth she hardly need have worried as Charlie was capable of doing most of the work himself. Like most men raised in rural Australia, Charlie was able to turn his hand to almost any mechanical task, finding a way to make do in any given situation was a way of life for country boys. They found a way to solve problems or were left stranded, sometimes a long way from home.

Not only was Charlie the right man for the job, so was his car. The big Hudson was a seven passenger touring car with a powerful six cylinder engine. It wasn't called a Super Six for nothing! The front seat and rear seats were permanently fixed in the car but it was common on such vehicles to have a small pair of fold out, or "jump" seats between them. These "jump seats" folded out of the floor and provided the accommodation for the two extra passengers that made the car a "seven passenger" phaeton.

Modifications to the Hudson were numerous to prepare it for the arduous trek the group was about to undertake. Charlie had only a couple of weeks to get everything done and he needed to make sure it would all fit in and on the Hudson. More than that, the car had to be able to deal with unexpected consequences of such an outback adventure, so they would need to carry extra fuel and water in addition to their normal day to day requirements.

Quite apart from preparing the vehicle, Charlie also had to contend with family members and friends constantly asking him why he would undertake such a crazy trip. It was, after all, only a little over 20 years since the first motorised vehicle of any kind had successfully made the dangerous journey up through the centre of Australia.

"Why would you charge off into the desert where there are almost no roads and what's more, do it with three ageing women?" was a common query from those around him.

"They are paying me good money at normal taxi rates," was his immediate reply, "Besides it will be quite an adventure. The ladies want their adventure and I can't think of anyone better equipped to provide it for them. It has all been decided, we leave on June 20."

—

Miss Beal busied herself with her own preparations while Charlie Heard was re-jigging his Hudson. Imagine how she must have pondered over what to take and what to leave at home. Even though she had offered to have Charlie's taxi equipped for this long journey, there would still be limitations to how much each passenger could logically take with them.

Charlie was offered good money to drive Miss Beal and her two companions on this outback adventure, but she knew such a trip would incur all sorts of extra costs over and above normal driving.

"I will cover the cost of all hotel accommodation where we can utilise it," she told Mr. Heard. "The same goes for telegrams back to your family, to let them know how we are getting on."

Wherever fuel costs were greater than the average Geelong price, Miss Beal also offered to pay the difference. In addition, the Beal account was to take care of all food costs and the camping gear for those many times when they would be nowhere near civilisation.

How could Charlie refuse? Everything was being taken care of, all he had to do was drive the unusual party safely to Darwin and back!

Charlie drew up a list of tasks that needed attention before the expedition was to leave on June 20. The Hudson would need a full and thorough service for the 7000 mile round trip in extreme

The Hudson fully kitted out for the expedition. Two forty gallon tanks were mounted, one on each running board, for extra water and fuel. Charlie made a bracket that fitted to the driver's side running board to hold all of the tents, poles and other camping equipment. A rack was added to the rear to carry a trunk holding the women's clothes, bedding and more camping gear along with a roll of coconut netting for traversing sandy tracts and even a wash up bowl.

conditions. Everything needed greasing and the engine, gearbox and differential oil was flushed and replaced with new oil. The same applied to the water in the radiator. A good flush and refill was required and a thorough check to make sure there weren't any leaks. Lights, brakes and springs were also checked in detail in an endeavour to eliminate any possible causes of unfortunate break down.

Extra fuel and water would be needed on board to enable the Hudson to tackle the long stretches of outback roads where there were no services available. Two large tanks were made up, each of 40 gallons capacity and designed to fit on the running boards of the Hudson. One was for extra petrol, the other for water. The extra fuel tank was mounted on the driver's side running board, just forward of the driver's door. The water went in the same position on the passenger side with a tap fitted as low down as possible.

Charlie made up a bracket that ran the full length of the driver's side running board to hold the tents, poles and other camping equipment. The spare tyre was already mounted on the rear of the car, but an extra rack was added to carry a trunk holding the women's clothes, bedding and more camping gear. A long roll of coconut netting was also included for those times when they encountered soft sandy tracts that would normally result in a bogged vehicle. Charlie had thought of everything, even a wash up bowl to keep the camp somewhat civilised.

There was to be a designated place for everything needed for the trip. Charlie's clothes, tools and wheel chains were allocated to the front mudguard area forward of the water tank. The same position on the driver's side was to be home for camp chairs, a folding table, wet weather coats and boots.

Having taken up all the space on the driver's side running board, access to the vehicle would always be from the left side. Some items would need to go inside the car so Charlie made up a flat case to fit on the rear floor, covering the area where the jump seats were folded. With only three passengers and driver the jump seats wouldn't be needed on this trip. The flat case was the storage space for all of their cooking and eating utensils and it would be low enough that Miss Wilmot and Miss Glenny could rest their feet on top and still be comfortable. Naturally, Miss Beal would travel in the front passenger seat alongside Charlie. Somewhere in the car, Charlie found space to include Miss Beal's gramaphone, which would often be the only entertainment the group enjoyed, apart from their own company.

Getting all of this ready was no small feat and it all needed to be completed by June 18. That would leave Charlie just one day to test run the car with all equipment in place and make any minor adjustments before he headed off from Geelong on June 20, 1930.

■ Chapter
3

Departure

Eileen

Glenny arrived at Ada Beal's house on the same Friday that Charlie Heard was to leave Geelong. It was already close to midday when she pushed the gate open with a mixture of trepidation and excitement. The trip was really going to happen, even though it had seemed like a dream up until now. The two ladies spent the rest of the day packing up ready for departure the next morning, excitedly guessing at what they might experience along the way.

Lil Wilmot was travelling from Melbourne on the Warrnambool train and she would join the group at the Birregurra railway station, some 23 miles north of Lorne. It would be an early start for Miss Wilmot as the train was due in Birregurra by 10:00am Saturday morning.

—

There was a touch of excitement for Charlie as he finally packed the Hudson on Friday morning. Even though there was plenty to stow aboard he had it all done by 10:00 am. Everything fitted as planned and there was still space for each of the ladies' clothes and personal gear to fit in its allocated place. All the time Charlie was aware that he was only the driver and if Miss Beal wanted to change things around, then as long as it would still all fit, that would be fine with him.

For Charlie there was a sense of excitement tempered by the fact that he was saying goodbye to Hazel, Vemba, Norma, Dawn and Merv for at least three months.

"It's time for you to become the man of the house and look after your mother while I'm gone," Charlie told Merv. "You girls be sure to help out too," he added, as he clambered aboard the Hudson.

It was hard for Hazel to hold back the tears as Charlie climbed behind the steering wheel and started the big Hudson. Charlie dropped the gear lever into first and let the clutch out just as he had done every time he drove the car, but the extra weight of the loaded Hudson, combined with Charlie's mixed emotions, resulted in a lurching, bouncing launch. Slightly embarrassed, he had to quickly regain his and the car's composure, give one last wave to the family and he was away.

This was a momentous occasion for Charlie, a trip that he would remember for the remainder of his life. What lay ahead? How long will it take? Have I thought of everything? These were just some of the thoughts racing through his mind as he drove through central Geelong on his way to Lorne. Of course everyone else in Geelong was going about their daily business, no life-changing excursions for them today. Somehow Charlie felt a little special as a result.

"Look at everyone else drudging through their day while I'm off to Darwin," thought Charlie as he sat a little higher in the seat.

But the realisation that it would be three months before he saw his family again cooled his enthusiasm a little and he soon settled down to the task at hand. All he needed to concentrate on now was getting to Miss Beal's in Lorne by late afternoon and checking into the local hotel so he could rest up before an early start on Saturday morning. Down through Jan Juc and Anglesea he drove, hardly noticing the familiar passing scenery, until he reached the start of the Great Ocean Road just past Anglesea. Even this was familiar, as Charlie had worked on the road just after the Great War. Charlie drew the big Hudson up to the new toll-gate and paid his fee to use the twisting but wonderfully scenic road to Lorne. Rolling waves crashed onto the beach beside the road as he passed through Aireys Inlet, almost mocking him with the amount of water they carried to a futile end on the sand. Where he was headed there would be little water to see, so he gazed out across Bass Strait, absorbing the wide blue expanse as the Hudson purred along,

For several miles the Great Ocean Road twisted away under the tyres of the Hudson until he reached the exit toll-gate. Just one more twisty section remained before the road straightened and carried Charlie toward Lorne. Rattling boards on the bridge over the Erskine River startled Charlie a little as he was daydreaming of the adventure that lay before him.

—

The traffic on the Melbourne road outside his home usually meant Charlie was well awake by six o'clock in the morning, but it was much quieter in Lorne at that time of the day, so Charlie slept on in comfort. All the preparation and the emotions of leaving home had caught up and sleep was a welcome respite. Before turning in for the night Charlie had used his idle time to write a letter to Hazel and the family.

"I will post it first chance tomorrow," he thought, "It might make them all feel a little better to know I am thinking of them already, even though the trip is just beginning."

The alarm on Charlie's little wind-up travel clock jangled away at 6:30 am and suddenly Charlie was aware he was in unfamiliar surrounds.

"Better get used to this," he mumbled to himself as he wiped the sleep from his eyes, "It will be a long time before I get to sleep in my own bed again."

A hearty breakfast in the dining room of the hotel soon had Charlie feeling better and he was raring to go by the time he arrived at "Llandoo" at 7:30 am. Miss Beal and Miss Glenny were already up and about and greeted him with a hearty "Good morning, Mr. Heard", as he wheeled up to the front gate.

Excited chatter gave way to more serious tones as Charlie set about getting the Hudson loaded with the women's belongings. It was soon all stowed in the allocated spaces, bearing in mind that they needed to allow for Miss Wilmot's luggage once they reached Birragurra.

—

While Charlie loaded the Hudson, Miss Beal and Miss Glenny were busily occupied with a group of friends who had come to see them off. Amongst them was Mr. Jarrett who was given the important task of taking a photograph to capture the momentous occasion. He soon had them all lined up in front of the Hudson, Mr. Heard comfortably leaning up against the front mudguard with hands in his pockets and Miss Glenny to the left of him with her hand bag on her arm. Miss Beal took up her position in the passenger doorway of the Hudson, her arm supporting her on the open front door of the car. All of the friends then gathered in a line beside Miss Beal. Included in that group were Mesdames Armytage and Campbell, and Misses McIntosh, Armytage and Cox.

The crisp morning air of early winter meant most were dressed in long coats, Miss Beal in her favourite fur coat that she would wear for much of the time during the trip. Charlie wore his three quarter length double breasted winter coat and Miss Glenny was snug with a fluffy stole around her shoulders.

No doubt this would change when they headed into the outback, but at this time of the morning warmth was the most important thing. Just as the temperature was sure to change, so would the surrounds in which the group found themselves. The bushy surrounds of Lorne would be a welcome sight when the expedition came to an end, after weeks in the dry and dusty outback.

"Climb aboard," called Charlie, "Time we were on our way to Birregurra, we don't want to keep Miss Wilmot waiting and it's nine o'clock already."

The road from Lorne to Birregurra winds its way through the Otway Ranges to Benwerrin and Deans Marsh where a left turn takes travellers from the hills toward Victoria's rich Western District

Left to right: Eileen Glenny, Lil Wilmott and Ada Beal.

farming area. It's a scenic drive that had Miss Beal and Miss Glenny marvelling at the beautiful forest, interspersed in places with varieties of heath and wattle. Even Charlie thought this was an amazing part of the country, certainly a very enjoyable way to begin their long journey together.

The trip to Birregurra seemed to take no time at all and the Hudson was soon parked outside the railway station. A smiling Miss Wilmot was pleased to see her friends arrive on time and she was not long off the train herself. Charlie was only just beginning to load her belongings when there was a stifled shriek from Miss Wilmot.

"Oh, no," she cried, "I've left my fur rug on the train and it's now on its way to Deans Marsh!"

"Not to worry, I will have the station master call ahead and have them retrieve it, then send the rug onto Port Fairy where we are staying tonight," offered Charlie as he rushed into the station. He was soon back with the good news that the rug would be taken care of and would be sent on to Port Fairy on the next available train.

Ada Beal had Charlie stop at "The Reformer" office in Colac to tell them about their expedition because it would make a good story for the local paper.

"Thank goodness," Miss Wilmot sighed with relief.

Before leaving Birregurra, Miss Beal had Charlie call by the local bank so she could pick up a letter of credit. It would be foolhardy to carry a large amount of cash on the long trip, so the letter of credit would mean Miss Beal could access funds as she needed them along the way. With the finances taken care of, Charlie pointed the bonnet of the Hudson toward Colac and the little band of adventurers was now officially on their way.

With the Hudson humming along the highway to Colac and beyond, Charlie was settling in for the next leg when Miss Beal interrupted his daydreaming thoughts with a request to call by "The Reformer" office in Colac.

"I want to tell them about our expedition," she insisted, "it should make a good story for the local paper."

The stop-over in Colac also allowed Miss Beal to briefly catch up with another of her many acquaintances – a Miss Brien.

"Time to get moving again," called Charlie, "We need to be sure to reach Port Fairy tonight and that's another 88 miles away."

Miss Beal suddenly started giggling hysterically. Amid all the confusion surrounding the group Miss Wilmot had mistaken Miss Brien for Miss Glenny and was firmly insisting that she climb into the back seat. She soon realised her mistake, but the incident was sure to be relived many times when the trip was over.

Back on the road, the excited party passed by Lake Corangamite and through the twisty section of road into the Stony Rises to Camperdown, the next major town on the route, where a stop was made at "The Leura" for lunch. Charlie took the opportunity to post home his letter to the family and then it was back on the road to Terang and through the rich pastoral and dairying districts to Warrnambool. The day was wearing on when Warrnambool was reached shortly after 4:00 pm, but it is only a short drive from there to Port Fairy, so the ladies agreed a quick afternoon tea was in order and they would still reach Port Fairy by nightfall.

The "Star of the West Hotel" was to provide the night's accommodation for the group. Excitement was still running high for the women who intended to stay up late and go to a picture show.

"Not for me," advised Charlie, "I need to get my rest, there's a lot of driving ahead of us."

After dinner the group sat for a time in the sitting room at the hotel where Miss Beal met up with another familiar acquaintance, a Mr. Thompson, cousin to her friend Alex Thompson from Monivae. The ladies then adjourned to the picture show that Ada described as "rotten", no sense mincing words, she didn't like it!

Miss Beal had organised for someone to fetch Miss Wilmot's fur rug when it finally arrived on the midnight train. It had been successfully intercepted at Deans Marsh and re-assigned to Port Fairy. While the ladies "enjoyed" their picture show, Charlie rested up and wrote up the diary that he would religiously maintain throughout the trip. The final entry for the day was, "Total miles for the day only 122". There would be plenty more to add over the next three months.

Port Fairy to Adelaide

Loaded

with all of their luggage and equipment by 9:00 am on Sunday morning, the party clambered aboard and Charlie gave the Hudson its head on the road to Portland. First stop along the way was at the small settlement of Yambuk to take on fuel. The congregation was coming out of the local church as Charlie was fueling up and they were obviously intrigued by this heavily laden Hudson with its trio of women and sole male occupant, obviously heading off on a camping holiday somewhere. Little would they have realised just how far that camping holiday would take the group.

With a full load of petrol in the tank, the leg to Portland was resumed, and the destination was reached a little before midday. Charlie drove out onto the pier and made a quick tour around other local tourist sites such as the Henty's home, where the first settlement in Portland was based almost a century earlier.

Keen to make as many miles as possible, the highway to Heywood was soon rolling under the Hudson, where the promise of a sit-down lunch beckoned. It was 1:00 pm by the time Heywood was reached but a hearty roast chicken lunch soon satisfied the now hungry travellers.

"No time to waste," Charlie said as he interrupted their post-meal comfort, "we have to reach Mt Gambier today, so let's climb aboard and get moving."

The road to Mt Gambier winds its way through pretty forest country that Ada, Lil and Eileen enjoyed immensely. Lots of coloured parrots cavorting to and fro across the path of the Hudson kept them marvelling at their beauty. In what seemed like no time at all, they passed through Dartmoor and were crossing the border into South Australia. Soon the crater of the Blue Lake loomed into view, signalling their arrival in Mt Gambier.

Just as they did in Portland, Charlie took the ladies for a quick tour of the various lakes that are the main tourist attractions of Mt Gambier. All agreed the Blue Lake was the most spectacular, yet uncanny at the same time, so brilliantly blue that it seemed almost artificial, even though it was not at its brightest blue at this time of the year.

"What a pretty place," chimed all three women, slightly amused that they were thinking and saying the same thing in unison.

The need to camp overnight in the open was still a long way off and the comforts of the Mt Gambier Hotel awaited them on this occasion. The proprietor was quite a talkative chap, keeping the group entertained well into the night with tales of local folklore.

—

All members of the group slept well overnight, perhaps a little too well, as it was 9:30am by the time the Hudson was called into action the next morning. First stop was the Mt Gambier Police Station where Charlie needed to transfer the car licence from Victoria to South Australia before they went any further. Millicent was the next town on the itinerary, but before leaving Mt Gambier there was one more tourist attraction to visit. Whilst staying at the hotel, Charlie was told of the amazing "sump hole" in the Cave Gardens where the local townspeople threw their rubbish and it disappeared overnight as if by magic. This they had to see with their own eyes. The Cave Gardens Reserve turned out to be a shady, landscaped park surrounding a sinkhole, with steps leading some of the way down into a deep limestone cavern. The stream running through the cave eventually filters into the Blue Lake, so it was no longer used as a rubbish dump, and an impressive marble fountain had been placed in the Reserve, a bequest of Captain Robert Gardiner in 1883.

The road to Millicent was a pleasant surprise as it was the first "metal sealed" highway they had travelled on since leaving Lorne. Morning tea was high on the agenda as they pulled into the town, Charlie always fond of a hot cup of tea. On this occasion he was able to combine it with a delicious hot pie and even the ladies commented on these pies. They also purchased a quantity of fruit for use as snacks along the way.

Next stop was Beachport, for lunch, and then straight on to Robe where a longer stop-over was planned, including the inevitable afternoon tea. The longer break enabled telegrams to be sent home, telling family members and friends of their progress so far.

Kingston was the final stop for the day, but on the way into town there was a pause to pick some mushrooms growing by the roadside. These were combined with garfish and crayfish, purchased locally and prepared by themselves for the evening meal. Food was high on the list of important matters on these early days of the trip, knowing they would need to be more frugal and basic with their menu once they reached the outback.

—

The countryside soon turned barren and lifeless after leaving Kingston on June 23. Charlie was mindful of how much better it had looked back in the Birragurra area but the travelling was pleasant nonetheless, as the Hudson was positively purring along at 40-45mph over recently completed road works. Dry pipe-clay swamps, a dead emu and straggly old dilapidated fences dotted the landscape as the Hudson motored on toward Woods Wells at the start of the Coorong, that unique salt water lake that parallels the coastline without joining to the sea until it merges with the mouth of the Murray River.

A mob of seven emus attracted everyone's attention as they cruised along through the poor-looking countryside until they reached Woods Wells where the lunch stop was taken, in the form of delicious butterfish. Prolific bird-life joined them for lunch at this point. Swans, seagulls, ducks, pelicans, stiels and a wide variety of other interesting water birds obviously found the Coorong waters well-stocked with food.

The day had proved most interesting, despite the barren landscape, by the time they reached Meningie on the edge of Lake Albert at 3:30 pm. Having made good time during the day there was ample leisure time to inspect the impressive local war memorial before settling down at the hotel. Other visitors and locals provided entertainment and conversation in the evening, but there was bad news regarding the conditions further along.

"You're a game lot heading up into that country in a car like that," opined one well-travelled resident. "I hope you're well-equipped for emergencies, there's not much in the way of services up through the middle."

Privately, Charlie was now a little worried. Had he anticipated all their needs? He re-assured himself that he had prepared as well as could be anticipated and tried to put it out of his mind. Miss Beal was also a little concerned, but she had set herself to do this trip and was now quite confident in Mr. Heard's capabilities. She steeled herself to go on regardless. Part of her reason for undertaking the trip was to prove that women could cope with such potential adversity – and to satisfy her own considerable sense of adventure. Maybe the best part was just beginning to unfold. The next few weeks of their adventure would tell the full story soon enough.

—

There was much excitement in the Hudson as the group motored out of Meningie at 9:00 am on June 24. Adelaide was to be the next stop but first they had to follow the Murray River for some distance before crossing it by punt at Wellington. A hotel on the banks of the river provided the day's first break for morning tea, but Charlie was soon anxious to resume travelling, as there was a significant climb up Mt Barker to be negotiated before they would reach Adelaide late in the afternoon. With so much weight strapped to the Hudson it would be a testy climb up the 1800 feet to Mt Barker and an even more difficult task coming down the other side, off Mt Lofty and into Adelaide. The increased weight would mean Charlie would have to rely more on the gears and less on the brakes if they were to make the descent safely.

The breathtaking drive through gum tree country to Mt Barker provided plenty of opportunities for taking photos and all four snapped away happily. Lunch was taken on reaching Mt Barker and the Hudson had the chance to cool down and recover from the steep climb. The road over Mt Lofty to Adelaide was in surprisingly good condition, but still Charlie drove very carefully. All that weight on the car meant the smell of hot brakes would soon become unbearable if he had to use them too often on the downhill run into Adelaide. The gearbox was certainly given a solid workout as a result.

In due course the Hudson rolled off the bottom of the hills and into central Adelaide where they had to search a little to find a hotel that had garage space for the car. The Black Bull Hotel proved one of only a few that were suitable and the group found it quite comfortable. Charlie and the ladies were taken with a sign that the proprietors had set up that read:

The Black Bull Hotel was one of few that provided garage space for the car.

"The bull is tame, so fear him not,
So long as you can pay your shot.
When money's gone and credit's bad,
That's what makes the bull go mad."

The sheer size of Adelaide, compared to the mostly small villages they had passed through on the way, had all four travellers marvelling at its superb array of department stores, among them Myers, Foys and Edments. All of these major shops crowded into the narrow space of downtown Rundle Street added to the busy atmosphere that was fascinating to the travellers. Adding to the clamour of the city were unemployed musicians, busking on almost every city corner.

High on the agenda, once settled in Adelaide, was a visit to the Post Office to pick up and post mail and then a visit to a Chinese store rewarded Ada with a supply of lychee and popplenuts. Following dinner at the Hotel, the ladies headed off to a session at the "talkies", but they came away disappointed.

"More inferior entertainment," muttered Miss Beal.

—

Perhaps there was a little more to Ada's feisty disappointment with the picture show the previous evening, as she was off to the Commercial Bank first thing next morning to seek out a recommendation for a dentist she might visit to have an aching tooth checked. Mr. Webb attended to Miss Beal's tooth by removing it from her jaw, with some difficulty, effectively fixing her pain and ensuring she was not so sprightly for the remainder of the day.

Charlie had planned out his part of the expedition with meticulous attention to detail, part of which included leaving it until the group reached Adelaide to purchase some of their required camping gear. Ada's disposition provided the opportunity for the rest of the group to go shopping for the camping gear and for grocery provisions for the next part of the journey. Bell camp tents, bedding and kitchen utensils were amongst the equipment allocated their pre-determined places in and on the Hudson. Meanwhile Lil and Eileen did the grocery shopping while Ada endured her

The railway station in Adelaide was virtually a mini city in its own right. The magnificent building housed fruit stalls, newsagent, a dining hall that was billed as handsome and magnificently appointed. It even had its own barber shop – all part of Railway Commissioner William Alfred Webb's grand plan. Webb's grand vision almost bankrupted the state and he became very unpopular. He returned to the USA in 1930.

Even as early as 1930 Adelaide was known as the City of Churches. Partially hidden behind the tree in this photo from Charlie Heard's personal photo album is St Peter's Anglican Cathedral in central Adelaide.

Another view of the Adelaide Railway Station that was reputed to have cost over £800,000 to build, an enormous amount in 1928 when it was completed.

misery alone in the hotel. By this time it was nearing closing time so shop attendants scattered in a flurry to fulfill the ladies' shopping requirements. Like beasts of burden they returned to the hotel laden with goods and ravenously hungry for their evening meal.

Miss Beal was emerging from her desolation after tea so the trusty gramophone was brought out to provide an evening of pleasant music that everyone enjoyed by the warm fire. Soon the comfort level of each night's accommodation would change dramatically so all four travellers relished this last night in Adelaide.

■ Chapter 5

From Adelaide to Outback SA

The ladies must have been trying to make their last

taste of civilised living last as long as possible as it took longer than most of the days up to this point to check out of the Black Bull Hotel. By 11:00 am the Hudson was on its way up the Main North Road and out of Adelaide, bound for Clare, via Stockport. The road conditions were good until a detour was required at Stockport. Lunchtime saw the welcome signs of Tarlee appearing in front of the group so a stop to proceedings was called for refreshments. The hilly country leading to Clare delighted the party and the road conditions remained fair until they arrived in Clare. Tonight it was to be Bentley's Hotel that would provide the accommodation, so Ada, Lil and Eileen would enjoy at least one more night in comfortable surrounds.

Dinner time brought a new experience for Eileen as she had never before tasted green olives. Ginger ale was poured for supper and unheralded entertainment supplied by a pessimistic woman who insisted on attaching herself to the travelling group.

"Where are you lot going then?" she asked in an invasive manner.

Ada took a small step backwards before replying, "All the way to Darwin and back." She said.

"You're mad," snapped the uninvited guest, "there's nothing out there, you'll perish in the outback. Wouldn't catch me doing anything dangerous like that."

Despite her apparent aversion for the outback the miserable woman persisted, warming a little to the idea of taking a taxi ride to Darwin and back.

"I hope your son is a good mechanic and knows how to handle that big car of yours." She added. "I bet you will see some amazing things along the way."

It was all Miss Beal could do to contain her composure before she quickly corrected the woman.

"Mr. Heard is not my son," she offered, "I have retained the services of his taxi for the trip and, yes, I do feel he is more than capable of getting us safely there and back."

"My goodness, you really are determined to do this trip aren't you?" replied the woman, "How I wish I had the gumption to embark on such an adventure."

All the while that this conversation was taking place between the women, Charlie was sitting in the background, quietly smoking, until a hotel staff member pointed out that smoking was prohibited in this section of the hotel. Embarrassed, Charlie moved to extinguish his cigarette, but was stopped in his tracks by another hotel patron who calmly walked over to the sign prohibiting smoking and promptly removed it.

"There," he stated in bold terms, "Now you can smoke all you like as it is no longer prohibited."

Charlie continued to smoke and wasn't confronted again.

—

It was Saturday June 28 when Clare slipped away in the rear view mirror of the Hudson and the expedition made its way to Melrose for lunch. Here they shared their meal with a wide variety of birds and animals, including a pair of tame cockatoos that chattered away merrily while riding on the waitresses shoulders. A kookaburra, a plover, several white rabbits and a dog all took their turn at attracting the party's attention to their particular corner of the yard, hoping perhaps that they might get to share a left-over morsel of lunch.

From Clare the road to Port Augusta took the loaded Hudson over the lower part of the Flinders Ranges. Passing by Mt Remarkable the weather conditions became very windy, blowing up a dust storm of such density that the mountain disappeared into the dust cloud. It was an indicator of very dry conditions on the westward side of the range where the countryside deteriorated rapidly to bare paddocks with devastating affects on stock. All were very lean, almost in a state of starvation.

The Hudson wheeled along marvellously in the warmer conditions, bringing the arrival time in Port Augusta all the way forward to 3:00pm. That left plenty of time to find a clean hotel for the night and some time to rest up before the evening meal. Charlie was content to get an early night, but the trio of ladies was off for a night at the "talkies", where "The Gold Diggers on Broadway" was showing.

Movie technology was still basic so projection equipment wasn't always reliable and the speech was often out of synchronization with the picture. The projectionist simply held a white sheet of paper in front of the lens until the picture caught up with the words.

—

All the heavy weight was telling on the Hudson's suspension, so Charlie called a halt to progress for another day at Port Augusta in order to have the front springs strengthened. This was achieved by having an additional leaf added to each spring that Charlie raided from an old wreck.

The extra break provided the opportunity for a walk around town on a glorious day, thanks to a cool southerly breeze coming in off the Spencer Gulf. Later in the afternoon the heat took over and brought with it hordes of annoying mosquitoes. The ladies sought shelter from both by going to church in the evening, after which Miss Beal spent considerable time in conversation with the clergyman. Back at the hotel, the last night in civilisation was somewhat spoiled by the incessant barrage of mosquitoes and the ladies were all up and out of bed early on Monday June 30 as they needed to prepare for their first venture into the real outback. Supplies, including meat, bread and other provisions were purchased first thing and Miss Beal made the local bank her next call as soon as the shopping was completed. The manager was an obliging fellow, agreeing to change Miss Beal's cheque even though it was not yet opening time.

Everything was loaded on board the Hudson, now fitted with its uprated springs, ready to tackle the vast outback. "Bookaloo Station" was the intended destination on this first day out of Port

The extra weight was telling on the Hudson so Charlie raided an old wreck in Port Augusta for extra spring leaves.

Augusta. Early into the day the group met up with an elderly man along the route who insisted that he share his damper with them. The outback roads weren't clearly marked so a stop was made at "Junapinna Station" to check directions.

The Paxton family owned "Junapinna", but the parents were away so their son and the housekeeper had been left in charge of the 55 year old wattle and daub homestead with drop log corners. They welcomed the visitors, offering them afternoon tea and a history lesson on the station for entertainment. They learned that "Junapinna" was the second largest station in South Australia, covering an area of two million acres.

The vagaries of life in the outback soon became apparent as Mr. Paxton Junior related how their normal average rainfall for the year was very poor.

"Usually we get seven inches, but the total so far this year is only two inches," drawled the lanky Mr. Paxton.

"The whole property is very dry. In a normal season we would carry up to 75,000 sheep, but the drought conditions mean it is only carrying 5000 at the moment."

Several quandong trees were growing about the homestead. These are unique to outback Australia, but still not common. Their tiny, golf ball size fruit having its own peculiar taste with only a thin layer of flesh over a hard, round, dimpled shell. The fruit in its raw form is quite tart to taste but responds well to sprinkling with sugar and makes quite delicious pies. Mr. Paxton also showed the group some serviette rings that had been carved from the hard Myall wood and then polished to reveal their beautiful dark colour.'

First camp at Bookaloo, South Australia.

Having determined the right way to go, the rest of the drive to "Bookaloo" was uneventful and all four were able to send telegrams home on arrival at the tiny settlement.

At "Bookaloo" the camping gear came out for the first time. A list of duties was agreed upon with Lil delegated to hold the tent poles while Charlie erected the bell tents. Eileen was to fold down the back of the front seat in the Hudson to make a bed for Miss Beal and herself and Ada prepared a fire and did the cooking of the evening meal. Charlie's other chores included setting up the tables and stools, Miss Beal's chair and unpacking the rest of the kit. As darkness descended Charlie pumped up the pressure in the Coleman lamp and it was lit for the first time, adding a warm and generous glow to the campsite. The first day in the outback came to a satisfying end for the whole party, congratulating themselves for working so well as a team.

—

Being a city girl, Miss Wilmot wasn't too sure about sleeping out in the bush for the first time. She had little sleep, listening to every strange sound and imagining wild animals and snakes all around that might make this her last night on earth. But eventually dawn broke and Lil had reason to wake in a happier mood, today July 1, she was to celebrate her birthday in the outback. Maybe that was part of the reason Charlie was less than happy with the packing up arrangements after breakfast. Where everything had gone to plan the evening before in setting up the camp, now nothing seemed to go back in place so easily.

"I hope we get better with practise," moaned Charlie, "We'll have to do this plenty of times before the trip is over."

First stop on this day was to be Woocalla where bread and some other supplies were to be purchased. Soon after leaving Woocalla the travellers came across more outback adventurers who were having their share of problems. Mr. Preston and Mr. Murray were travelling together but the Prestons' car was giving trouble. Charlie was able to carry out a simple repair to get them going again with fencing wire and a handful of tools. A tip of the hat and a firm handshake was the only payment needed and they were on the way again. These two parties were also heading for Darwin, so they all felt reassured that they weren't the only intrepid travellers taking on the outback.

Charlie gave the Hudson its head along what he thought was the right track but soon realised they were going in the wrong direction. The big tourer was turned around and before long the party was back on the right track, reaching Wirappa in time for lunch. Here Miss Beal brightened the day for a couple of local girls by giving them some chocolate, in return for which they offered her some goats milk.

Camp was set up early on this day to give everyone some time to write letters home while listening to Miss Beal's gramophone. By now Charlie was becoming a little homesick for Hazel, but the arrival of the two other travelling parties provided a distraction and they were invited to spend the night camped in the same area.

—

Fellow outback travellers also heading for Darwin were the Prestons and the Murrays, who were travelling in this 1927 Dodge Model 124 sedan on the left and 1924 Buick 6 Tourer on the right.

The 1924 Buick, 1927 Dodge and Charlie Heard's Hudson. Note how much larger the Hudson is compared to the other two cars.

Everyone had just settled into bed when heavy rain set in and it kept up incessantly right through the night. The grey dawn revealed an important lesson for the campers – don't pitch your tents in a low-lying area. Everything was wet; tents, beds, clothes, shoes – everything!

Ada was adamant that they should move to higher ground as soon as possible as it was still raining, making breakfast preparation quite a task. The rain made packing up a testing chore as well, but at least the three travelling parties were able to assist each other in getting to the higher ground. All became bogged in the attempt but Charlie was able to fit chains to his wheels and get free of the sticky mud. Then he used his coir matting, tied together as a makeshift tow-rope, to pull the others free. Lil opted to work in her bare feet, Eileen wore her shoes without stockings and Miss Beal chose to stay clear of the worst of the operation by staying out of the way in the car. At last all three cars and their contents were moved to higher ground and the rain finally abated at 10:00 am.

The deluge had turned the track into twin rivulets of water, making it very hard to progress with any speed. As it was the water and mud was splashing everywhere, often over the bonnet of the Hudson and even going right over the top of the car at times. The churning mud and water caught Charlie off-guard for a moment and all of a sudden the Hudson was bogged. Fortunately the Murray and Preston parties weren't far behind and were able to assist in freeing the Hudson from its muddy trap, but the going was very slow and only 25 miles were covered for the day.

Charlie elected to pitch camp early to give them all a chance to get some of their gear and clothes dry before nightfall. The Murrays and Prestons followed suit and once more camped alongside, just in case there was more rain through the night.

Outback camp, South Australia, note the chains on the rear wheel of the Hudson, necessary to gain traction on the rain soaked track.

As darkness descended on the camp it revealed a clear night sky dotted with stars and everyone breathed a sigh of relief. Mr. Preston came for a visit to Miss Beal's camp in the evening and they all enjoyed the magnificent starlit sky. Once again the gramophone was brought out for entertainment and everyone in the vicinity enjoyed symphonic music in the middle of the outback in the dead of night.

—

A glorious sunny morning greeted the travellers the next day and they were soon on their way to Kingoonya Sheep Station, following the railway line to rendezvous with a scheduled fuel stop that had been pre-arranged with the Shell Oil Company. There was no Shell Depot at Kingoonya railway siding, only a Post Office and a couple of sheds and railway homes, but there was a supply of fuel waiting at the railway station "for a travelling party". However no amount of talking by Charlie Heard could convince the station master that his was in fact the designated "travelling party".

"I suggest you continue on to Kingoonya Station", advised the uncooperative station master, "You should be able to get some fuel there."

Charlie was less than happy about the situation, but felt powerless to do anything about it. All they could do was head for the station and hope that they had enough fuel to get there. For what seemed like an eternity the Hudson purred along toward the station, all the time Charlie was on edge, waiting for that fatal engine splutter that would indicate their worst fears were being realised. Charlie kept shifting in his seat in anticipation, but tried not to reveal how anxious he really was

The same three vehicles in outback South Australia. The three parties camped together for two nights in a row, enduring heavy rainfall and slow progress.

about running out of petrol before they reached the station.

Just when it seemed they must surely run out, the station buildings loomed into view. There was a communal sigh of relief from all on board as the Hudson rolled into the homestead yard. There was little more than a cup-full of petrol in the tanks, they wouldn't have made it more than a few hundred yards further.

Kingoonya Station was owned by a Mr Taylor, who was occupied in the nearby woolshed, when Charlie's taxi drove into the yard. He wandered over to the homestead to greet the unannounced visitors and to see what they might be needing.

"Any chance we could buy some petrol from you?" asked Charlie in a hopeful voice. "There was supposed to be a consignment for us at the railway station, but the station master claimed it was for another party and we could not take delivery. He suggested there might be some available here."

"I'm convinced that fuel was meant for us," added Miss Beal, "I arranged it all before we left Victoria and was advised the local Shell agent would have a supply available for us. We now know there is no Shell agent at Kingoonya, but I am still convinced it was our petrol. I will be making some pointed inquiries when I get home," she added.

"Well, no problem," offered Mr Taylor, in his typically outback friendly tone. "We can spare you some fuel, pull over there by the sheds where the drums are stored and we'll get you fixed up."

Whilst there was jubilation amongst the ladies, Charlie could only think of what might have happened if they had run out of fuel when still miles from Kingoonya.

"You are so kind," responded Miss Beal, "Thank you very much. I don't suppose you might have some bread we could purchase as well, would you?"

"Better check with the wife on that score," came the reply, "She's over in the house."

Just as Mr Taylor made this suggestion, Mrs Taylor emerged from the house and was making her way toward the Hudson when there was a flurry of excitement from the back seat.

"I know you," gasped Miss Glenny from her seat, "We went to school together."

"Eileen Glenny!" shrieked Mrs Taylor, "What on earth are you doing way out here?"

"I might ask you the same thing!" replied Miss Glenny, amid much excited laughter.

Such a chance meeting meant an immediate change to plans for the next 24 hours. They couldn't resume their journey without giving the two school friends a chance to catch up on all that had happened in their lives since their school days.

"You must all stay for the night," said Mrs Taylor, "Come into the house and get cleaned up, we'll get some tea under way. This calls for a celebration."

The excited women chatted on for hours into the night and everyone was more than happy to take advantage of the steaming hot bath, home cooked meal and all around kindness that was shown to Miss Glenny and her travelling friends.

Ada was keen to catch up on any news from back home and noticed that Mrs Taylor was using some old Victorian newspapers for the bath heater. She was quick to ask if she could scan through

Relaxing at Kingoonya Station – Ada Beal, Miss Eileen Glenny and her school friend Mrs Taylor.

these newspapers and any others that might be on hand. While flicking through the Melbourne "Sun" from a few days before, Miss Beal suddenly gave a little, excited gasp.

"Well look at this!" she said, "One of the photos taken as we left my cottage in Lorne has ended up in the newspaper."

The cheery conversations went on well into the night, during which time the travelling party learnt all about Kingoonya Station. It was a huge acreage, as were most of the stations of this period, over three million acres in fact and normally stocked with 58,000 sheep. Even with those large numbers this still equates to 20 acres per sheep and being such a dry year, the number of sheep being shorn was down on normal years. The station was only employing eight men instead of the usual twenty and there was very little grass to be seen.

—

Everyone was up early and eating breakfast by 7:00am the next morning, July 4. The expedition was moving into its 15th day since leaving Lorne. Mr and Mrs Taylor loaded them up with a lot of supplies, including a generous supply of mutton as they were leaving.

The Hudson was still running beautifully, but during the day Charlie was distracted by a new noise emanating from under the front of the car. Every so often there was a crunch as if metal was grinding against metal in a manner not normal with movement of the suspension. A halt was called while Charlie investigated, only to find a broken front spring. It wouldn't stop their progress but

Charlie sits on the ground after checking the front springs on the Hudson, only to find one was broken.

Charlie decided to bind it up with wire to prevent further damage and a little more care was required while driving over any rough sections of track.

While Charlie was tending to the spring, the ladies took time to soak up all the delights of the outback environment. Overhead several wedge tailed eagles soared and hovered on thermal currents and all around they started noticing more and more flowers emerging in the desert. Amongst the many varieties of plants the ladies noticed pink daisies, pussy tail grass, blue geranium, blue salt bush and yellow acacias.

Despite this minor setback with the broken spring, the party managed to cover 140 miles before setting up camp for the night, just two miles short of their target for the day. Miss Beal busied herself with cooking some of the delicious mutton chops supplied by Mrs Taylor and all four enjoyed listening to her gramophone and writing letters home to loved ones.

Camped in the South Australian outback.

■ Chapter

6

Coober Pedy and Alice Springs

There was excitement in the air as the camp was packed up this morning

as today Coober Pedy was to be the destination and it was a relatively short 16 mile drive to get there, but the surrounding landscape was covered with gibber stones, like giant cobbled pavement with occasional dwarf shrubs here and there. Underneath the gibber plains was sandstone, once hidden under the sea and now containing gems – opals. Everyone was keen to reach this unusual town where most of the inhabitants live in dug out houses that are roomy and cool with little furniture. Usually seats and tables were simply dug out of the walls. In fact, on arrival at 11:00 am, they learned that "Coober Pedy" is Aboriginal for "one who lives underground" and that the township was established in 1915.

All of the mining is carried out underground and the dug out houses are practical as there is also a scarcity of timber for building in this barren environment. The whole party went shopping for gifts and supplies at Santungs Store, which was also the petrol depot and Charlie was pleased to obtain some opals from a miner to take home for his beloved Hazel. Miss Beal was also in an opal buying mood, gathering some for herself, along with a ring each for Eileen and Lil as a memento of their trip.

While the shopping was being attended to, Charlie was surprised and relieved to be able to have the broken spring replaced in the Hudson at a local workshop. There was a lot of rough terrain between here and Alice Springs and he wasn't looking forward to nursing the Hudson along with a faulty suspension for any longer than absolutely necessary.

Mrs Taylor had given Miss Beal a letter of introduction to a Miss Barrington before they left Kingoonya. She used this to procure accommodation in one of the dug out homes owned by local opal buyer Mr Burford, where travellers were made welcome to stay. Mr Burford was away at the time. The dug out home was very comfortable with snowy white blankets and a nice spring bed.

The English cricket results were coming through on the wireless and the group members were encouraged to join some locals in listening to it until midnight, but they declined in favour of extra sleep. Miss Beal was very concerned that they might be delayed at some point if any one of them caught a cold so she instituted a strict rule. Each party member was only allowed two sneezes per day. During this evening Miss Glenny was seized with a strong desire to sneeze, but having already used her "two per day" allocation had to creep away outside where she delivered four more as quietly as she could on her own.

—

Miss Beal was up and about very early on Sunday morning as the weekly food supply arrived in

Coober Pedy at midnight on Saturday and she was eager to get an early start on replenishing their stocks. Once that was taken care of the Hudson wheeled out of the opal town at 9:00 am. It was a very rough track that bounced the travellers around inside the tourer, but they made relatively good time despite the lack of a comfortable ride. Along the way a partly tame dingo was sighted but every endeavour to photograph it ended in failure. By the time they camped in a picturesque, but mosquito infested, dry creek bed they had covered 109 miles. The wonderful stew that Ada cooked up for the party that night was most welcome, teeming with vegetables and piping hot – if only they could enjoy it without having to constantly swat mosquitoes.

–

Coober Pedy Post Office.

The camping gear stayed on the Hudson in Coober Pedy as the passengers enjoyed the hospitality of the absent Mr Burford in his dug-out home.

Coober Pedy fuel depot with "Plume" sign on the side of the building.

Ada was busily cooking again bright and early the next morning, chops, eggs and bacon on the menu and all devoured in time to pack up the camp and be under way again by 8:00 am. The road wandered about much more in 1930 than it does today, but that didn't stop them from aiming for Oodnadatta by day's end. The travelling was through very harsh country with little growth evident in any form, just miles of brown ironstone gibbers.

Beautiful gum trees with snowy white trunks were evident along the edges of the dry creek beds, indicating that there must be some moisture down there somewhere.

Central Australian indigenous tribes knew this secret, they would often dig a soak-hole, or well, in the bottom of such creeks and the hole would gradually fill with water. It could take hours for a hole to fill with water, but it

Partly tamed kangaroo, just before Oodnadatta.

would be enough to sustain life in this barren outback environment. Europeans soon learnt to do the same, but not so well known is the fact that kangaroos, wallabies and horses could also dig a soak, but cattle were never known to dig for water.

The hours seemed to roll by very slowly through the day, punctuated occasionally by the sighting of kangaroos and the skeletons of long dead animals. Numerous birds and delicate wildflowers also provided some relief from the desert terrain and the ladies managed to pick and press some of the flowers to take home.

Here and there along the way, closer to Oodnadatta, the group started noticing large sheets of glassy looking gypsum that is peculiar to this area. In fact it was so clear and large in formation that it could actually be substituted for glass in those outback areas where it was too expensive to transport real glass all the way in from the large cities.

Eventually a row of buildings alongside the north-south strip of railway line confirmed that Oodnadatta was coming into view. There was only one hotel, the railway depot, Post Office, a store, a few houses and less than 100 people in Oodnadatta, but it was a welcome sight after the dreary landscape they had been driving through all day. There was also a medical hostel run by the Australian Inland Mission, started by John Flynn, with staff members A Calderwood, C Grace Bayley and Olive Ramsey.

It was now 4:00 pm and there were welcome hot baths available for a reasonable price at the hotel. Nobody complained about the strong sulphur smell that accompanied the bore water that comes straight out of the ground at comfortable bathing temperature, but it was hard not to notice.

Transcontinental Hotel in Oodnadatta.

Not all river and creek crossings were dry, as this fellow traveller found out at the billabong near the Abminga ruins, north of Oodnadatta.

The hotel had installed a storage tank where the water is allowed to cool, giving patrons the option of a cool shower from the tank or a hot bath direct from the water main. Miss Beal thought the sulphur smell would be very trying for some people, but it didn't seem to bother her too much, perhaps because she was distracted by some beautiful birds in a cage that caught her eye at the hotel.

The railway line had previously terminated here at Oodnadatta, but recently it had been extended through to Alice Springs, taking with it some of the old-time glamour that it enjoyed as the last civilised outpost. The railway line had replaced the camel and the horse as the beasts of burden that carried forward necessities to Alice Springs, with only a very occasional motor car making the same journey. Life in the outback was changing and Charlie and his taxi were part of the reason for that change. More people were undertaking a trip to the outback to see some of the "real Australia".

With the extension of the railway to Alice Springs came the now well-known name for the train as "The Ghan". It is obvious the name is a shortened form of "Afghan" in recognition of the contribution made by the Afghan camel train drivers of the period. They were well recognised as the main form of transport to Alice Springs for bringing in supplies and since the train replaced the camel trains it was seen as appropriate to name it after them.

What is not so well-known is that there were two Ghan trains in the early days – the "Flash Ghan" and the "Dirty Ghan". The "Flash Ghan" made the trip to Alice Springs once a fortnight with sleeper and dining car included, while the "Dirty Ghan" was used for transporting supplies only.

Lambs fry and bacon greeted the travellers when they emerged for breakfast at 7:00 am on July 8. There was time to post some mail and purchase more supplies before climbing aboard their trusty vehicle once more. Dry barren scenery was really starting to dominate the landscape now and Charlie couldn't help but notice the large number of dead animals scattered amongst the sand, mulga scrub and salt bush. They were grim reminders of how prepared outback adventurers like themselves needed to be in order to survive if something were to go wrong. The stony plains extended from Oodnadatta to beyond Charlotte Waters, still more than a day's travel ahead of them, and then the track would turn sandy again to the Finke River and from there on to Maryvale Station. There was some difficult travelling ahead.

As the day wore on the temperature rose dramatically, causing the normally very reliable Hudson to start overheating. Charlie even found it necessary to pull over several times to let the radiator cool down. After covering a tiring 105 miles by late afternoon the decision was made to pitch camp in what Ada referred to as a "sandy and most uninteresting spot".

Meal preparation usually fell to Miss Beal and it was while preparing for the evening meal that she made an unpleasant discovery.

Afghan Crossing on the Finke River, note the wheel tracks in the soft sand.

Preparing to cross the Finke River.

Preparing to cross the Finke River at Afghan Crossing.

Some help from the local Aborigines was needed to get the Hudson through the soft sand.

"Has anyone seen the tripod," she enquired of the others.

All looked with blank faces but no response.

"Don't tell me we left it behind this morning," she groaned with more than a hint of disgust.

Another search of all their camping gear ensued, but all to no avail. The cooking would have to be carried out without the handy tripod on which their cooking pot was usually suspended over the fire. Nevertheless Miss Beal still prepared a sumptuous meal as she did with her usual efficiency.

The daily menu was based around quite a settled schedule. There were always early cups of tea on rising, followed by breakfast, usually around 8:00 am and then tea and a biscuit at 11:00 am. A break for lunch was timed for 1pm accompanied by more tea and then afternoon tea was taken at 4:00 pm. The evening meal was prepared as soon as camp was set up at the end of the day with yet more cups of tea and sometimes there would even be another kettle on the boil for a late cuppa at 10:00 pm.

—

More of the desolate country greeted the travellers when they set off on Wednesday July 9, bound for Charlotte Waters and on to Old Crown Station. Once again there was a lot of dead stock to be seen and more very dry country. In fact the party members saw very little in the way of live animals right through this stretch of the outback. The track passed through Stevenson Valley and Bloods Creek before the tableland stepped up a few miles south of Charlotte Waters and the character of the

Crossing the Finke River at Afghan Crossing, all hands on deck to get the Hudson through the soft sand and up onto the opposite side bank. The Dodge sedan just setting out on its crossing.

landscape changed a few miles to the north. Here there was less gibber plain and it was generally less stony with occasional sand hills. Mulga and scrub emerged as the Hudson continued further north.

Charlotte Waters came and went without stopping, a move that was later regretted when Miss Beal learned that it was one of the outstanding places to see, compared to other outback stations. The station featured buildings made of yellow stone with a high wall around a courtyard. It had also been a scene of much unrest from the local Aborigines when the telegraph station was first established some 60 years earlier, following the route marked out by the intrepid explorer John McDouall Stuart. Much of the road that the Hudson was following was originally blazed by that same explorer in the early 1860s. Other explorers such as Giles and Forrest passed through this area on their early treks through Central Australia.

The distance from Charlotte Waters to Crown Point Station was 18 miles, then another 20 miles to South Well, where Charlie had arranged a fuel drop by the cameliers. Charlotte Waters Station was named after Lady Charlotte Bacon whose son Harley Bacon was Officer in Charge of the Telegraph Line supplies. The road crosses the Finke River just below Old Crown Point Station. The country is occupied for only about a 120 mile wide strip through here as it is otherwise mostly inhospitable. The first Finke River crossing was at Yellow Cliffs, going from west to east, then east to west again only one mile further north. Both crossings are through very loose sand. A few miles from Yellow Cliffs, by the river bank, is the old homestead of Crown Point Station, that was turned into a store when the new homestead was established further south at New Crown Station, where the Finke River was bored to a depth of 900 feet and still it revealed a sandy bottom.

Lots of pushing to get the Hudson out of the sand in the Finke River crossing.

Laying matting across Finke River, damage to the photo makes it appear like a sand storm.

The first stop for the day was at Old Crown Station where the manager and his family provided Ada, Lil, Eileen and Charlie with a pleasant morning tea. The station was actually owned by that famous Australian grazier, Sir Sidney Kidman, but it was being closed down due to the endless drought. All the stock was being moved 80 miles to the west where there was more feed available.

The manager recounted tales of huge floods in the previous February and there had been a lot of tree damage along the Finke River, which was soon to figure some more in their navigation. He also told the group of a huge thunderstorm that had shaken the house to its very foundations and lasted for several hours. There wasn't any resulting rain from this storm, but many meteorites were found after it had passed. The manager even gave them a meteorite to keep, along with some topaz, retrieved from the Finke River after the February flood. Despite the huge flash flood that swept down the river, nothing but wild melons grew and there was a lot of damage to what little infrastructure existed along the road.

Notorious for its usually intermittent flow, the Finke River ran for nine months in 1920-21, when Alice Springs had 40 inches of rain. The "Afghan Crossing" on the Finke River had been well corduroyed prior to 1929 but that was all washed away in the 1930 flood. The Finke River flood of January 1930 also washed out the new rail bridge and derailed the train.

The "Afghan Crossing" of the Finke River at Crown Point extends along the river for 2-3 kilometres. Ralph Milner took the first flock of sheep across the river here with great difficulty in 1870. The 7000 sheep swam across in single file after they had camped by the river for five weeks waiting for the flood waters to subside. Milner made it all the way to Darwin to claim the $4000.00 reward for the feat, but he never collected it due to a change in the South Australian Government. Fifteen hundred of the sheep died from eating gastrolobium (deadly nightshade) near the Devils Marbles. Ralph also sold 1000 of the sheep to the flood-bound telegraph construction party near the Roper River. He reached Darwin with 2000 sheep still intact and they were apparently sold on arrival.

A mile or two north of the store at Old Crown Station are rocky hills and Cunningham's Gap through which the Finke River flows. The flat topped hill near the gap is Crown Point and it is visible for miles in any direction. The flat top is surrounded by sheer sides that are 100 feet high. They drop away suddenly and then spread out to blend into the surrounding ground. From a distance it looks like a crown, hence the obvious name.

At Cunningham's Gap the river bed was also the road, but that wasn't normally a problem, except when it flooded on those rare occasions. The ground continues to rise to over 2000 feet from Crown Point to Horseshoe Bend, over a distance of 28 miles.

Thanking the inhabitants of Old Crown Station for their hospitality, Charlie fired the Hudson and turned its big wire wheels to the track once more. For the next several hours they wound their way back and forth across the Finke River and its surrounding sand dunes. Five river crossings were made during the afternoon, before it was time to set up the camp for the evening, this time on the banks of the Finke, which was bereft of water, but lined with the finest of clean, soft sand. So soft and clean was this sand that it became a favourite place to camp for all outback travellers looking for a little more comfort, and wary of prickly ground often encountered elsewhere. The commonly encountered drought conditions also meant that there was little chance of being caught in a flash flood during the night. The Finke River is up to 200 yards wide in this area and the track runs mostly alongside of it, alternating at seven different crossings along the sixty miles of track between Charlotte Waters and Horseshoe Bend.

—

Deeper into the centre of the continent the intrepid travellers moved with each passing day. More difficult Finke River crossings were required today and Charlie's matting was needed on several occasions. Often even that wasn't enough and local Aborigines and even the ladies themselves were called on to push and pull to get the Hudson through the softest patches.

Seasoned outback motorists, of whom there were an increasing number by 1930, had already worked out clever ways of coping with the trying terrain. One trick in soft sandy river crossings, was to deflate the tyres slightly so that they were less inclined to "dig in", giving the tyre a greater footprint and consequently a little more traction.

Some of the crossings were corduroyed with branches to make it easier for motor cars to cross, but still it was vital to be carrying the matting as used by Charlie Heard, or at least a length of wire netting.

In this area the Finke is lined with eucalypts on both banks, fed only by the occasional water flow down the river that only occurred once or twice each year. Nevertheless it was well known for providing water from soak holes in the sand.

Finally the crest of a fairly high hill was reached and there below them on the Hugh River, just up from its junction with the Finke, was the small, but picturesque settlement of Horseshoe Bend. Such was the geography of this location that the station, actually called Engoordina, but always referred to as just Horseshoe Bend, almost appeared to be underneath the car as they looked down from the crest.

The cluster of buildings included a hotel, a low stone building with stone floors, plus a post office and store that acted as the main establishment for the station. The hotel was run by Mr Elliott, who also ran the station and store, and at the time it was the southern most licensed hotel in Central Australia. For many years the post office here was the mail exchange point for the camel teams. There is a grave just before the crest of the sand hill where a man died from thirst and starvation only a very short distance from the top. If he had made it to the top he would have seen the station and been saved.

The homestead provided primitive but clean accommodation for the night, a pleasant change from the many camps the group had now endured in the outback. The bath consisted of a tub and a bucket, but it was still most welcome and the lady of the house was a pleasant and very interesting woman. She was excited that her daughter was due home soon from one of the big public schools in Melbourne, but Mr Elliott did not enjoy the best of health. He suffered from a constant cough that worried him considerably and kept the visitors awake for most of the night.

—

Charlie fired up the Hudson at 9:00 am on Friday morning and the tourists were soon on their way, but not for very long. North of Horseshoe Bend are the rolling Depot Sand Hills that range for 20 miles from east to west. The track crosses these sand hills at right angles, 80 times up and down, in that 20 mile stretch and it crosses the Hugh River 10 times in that distance. The hills aren't loose sand, apart from where the track wends its way across, mostly they are covered with vegetation in the form of spinifex, with some other grasses and occasional desert oak trees. The sand hills can be avoided by using a longer track across the south west end of the hills, following the Hugh River, and joining the main track again just before Alice Well. This is a very picturesque route.

Two of these crossings of the Finke River were required soon after leaving Horseshoe Bend and they proved quite difficult. The owners of the homestead came to their assistance, which was most appreciated, but there was another problem about to become obvious. With all the confused activity surrounding the river crossings, Charlie had headed off in the wrong direction and they had covered some ten miles before the error was discovered. Fortunately Charlie carried a compass and that, combined with an accute sense of direction avoided what could have been a costly mistake.

Soon they were back on the right track, but confronted with more river crossings. After the difficulties experienced with the crossings earlier in the day, the ladies decided to walk across the river bed at each new crossing while Charlie drove the Hudson across.

At one of these crossings on the Alice Springs track, the group met up with a local character named Michael Terry. They spent some time talking with him about the track and what lay ahead. Mr Terry told them it was just a short 40 minute drive to Alice Wells, the next settlement. What they didn't know was that Michael Terry was also something of a practical joker. His short 40 minute drive was in fact more than two hours! They found out later that he was quite fond of deliberately misleading outback travellers in this way.

Michael Terry was actually on his way to Erldunda where his "Endeavour Expedition" left on

Camped at Alice Wells.

Last camp before Alice Springs, under the trees at Alice Wells.

July 19, 1930, bound for the Petermann Range. The trek he made was later to become the main road access into this part of Central Australia and Michael Terry became quite famous in his own right for blazing trails through many parts of the inland.

At the next crossing Miss Beal hailed a police constable who was travelling with his wife.

"It is alright Miss Beal", he called out, "We have come to meet you, my wife being anxious at your being late and we thought you might be short of water." The mounted trooper from Alice Well was Constable Jack Mackay, a very likeable and respected police officer who occupied the Alice Wells Police Station that was established in 1912. Many times he faced death from thirst in the dry inland. He unfortunately drowned while on holiday with friends when on his annual leave.

That night they all camped on an old camping ground that had been established by the explorer Earnest Giles under an historic tree, the largest they had seen while in Central Australia. Constable and Mrs Cameron, also from Alice Wells, spent the evening with the group and they all stayed up late listening to Miss Beal's and the Camerons' records until the "ghastly hour" of almost 1:00 am.

Once everyone had settled down to sleep for what was left of the night, Miss Beal found she was disturbed by the noisy snoring of the other members of the group.

"Eileen", she called out, ruffling her bedding at the same time.

"What's wrong?" queried Miss Glenny sleepily, as she struggled to emerge from her comfortable bedding.

"You're all snoring so loudly I can't get to sleep myself", she replied with a hint of laughter in her voice.

"You woke me to tell me that!" she curtly responded. "Go back to sleep."

Mule cart with its Aboriginal attendant at Alice Wells.

A camel string near Alice Springs. They were still required to deliver goods east and west of Alice Springs after the arrival of the Ghan Railway in 1929.

Everyone slept in their clothes overnight but by early morning it was icy cold. Charlie rose early and made hot tea for the others, which he served to them while they were still in bed. Once some bodily warmth had been gained, Miss Beal set about her usual morning duty of cooking a hot breakfast. Constable and Mrs Cameron acted as hosts to show them around the garden after breakfast and introduced the party to a new-born Aboriginal baby which Ada described as a "queer looking little thing". They watched donkeys drawing water from the well to water the garden and it was here at Alice Wells that the travellers saw their first herd of camels. Mrs Cameron gave Miss Beal some seeds from a Japanese passion fruit and the camp was all packed up ready for departure while the morning was still young.

Only two dry river crossings were required today as the Hudson taxi nudged its way ever closer to Alice Springs. In 1930 the main settlement was actually known as Stuart and it was situated some two miles from the Alice Springs Post Office. The entrance to Stuart was through the MacDonnell Ranges where the scenery was quite pretty, with beautiful white gums and plenty of long grass as the track passed through Heavitree Gap, leading into the township of Stuart. Heavitree Gap was named after Charles Todd, it was his second name. Todd was Postmaster General, Superintendent of Telegraphs and Government Astronomer for South Australia when the inland telegraph line was established.

View over Alice Springs shows the Catholic Church in the foreground and the MacDonnell Ranges in the background.

Alice Springs Railway Station was almost brand new having been built in 1929 when the railway extension from Oodnadatta to Alice Springs was completed.

Shortly after this time Stuart was officially gazetted as Alice Springs and all of the official buildings were moved to this part of the township. In the Todd River at Alice Springs there was an eight gallon petrol drum that was set into the sandy river bottom with a camp oven lid on the top. This was a soak for general public use, complete with a pannikin inside on a wire hook. The drum was usually half full of cool, clear water.

Once the travellers had settled into Eileen and Joseph Kilgariff's Stuart Arms Hotel, mail was collected and telegrams sent from the post office at the Telegraph Station where Ernest Allchurch was in charge. He filled that role from 1924 until the Telegraph Office closed in 1932. He was first there in a subordinate position from 1905.

All four tourists thoroughly enjoyed being back in civilisation once more, where there were comfortable beds to sleep in. At last they had reached the true centre of Australia.

■Chapter

7

On to Darwin

Alice

Springs in 1930 consisted of a hotel, two stores, two houses, two huts, a police station and residence, court house, cells, plus a school and garden. Ah Hong's vegetable garden and eating house was also established plus another cottage. The local storekeeper's name was George Fogarty. The Telegraph Station and its cluster of associated buildings was located nearby, but separate from the town of Stuart, as Alice Springs was known, until the whole township area was proclaimed "Alice Springs".

The white population of Alice Springs in 1930 was less than 600. Fogarty's store shared with the pub the distinction of being the hub of the emerging town. Here you could get supplies and organise transport on camels, trucks or horses. Charlie Meyers had the saddle shop and his wife ran the boarding house that was said to have the "best table in Alice Springs". Minister Tom Lithgow of the Australian Inland Mission had a shack in the main street of Alice Springs in front of Johanssen's home, opposite Adelaide House. Mrs Meyers' boarding house also provided meals and the Stuart Arms Hotel was opened by Joseph Kilgariff. The Underdown brothers had also opened their store in August 1929 in Gregory Terrace. They had a store previously at Oodnadatta, but

Camel trains make their through Heavitree Gap, bringing timber into Alice Springs.

moved to Alice Springs on completion of the railway line, where they then competed with Fogarty's store. Pearl Burton arrived in May 1929 to run the school that was almost completed when Charlie Heard and his passengers visited Alice Springs. The school actually opened on September 22, 1930.

While staying in Alice Springs, Miss Glenny met a priest whom she had known in Papua. He had been transferred to Alice Springs from Port Moresby and now tended to a parish that covered 2500 miles. The Alice Springs Catholic Church was established by the Missionaries of the Sacred Heart in 1929, with Father Long coming from mission work in New Guinea to be the first Parish Priest. He told them of some of his exploits in this huge new environment where he had managed to cover some 2000 miles in a month and been bogged twenty times.

Charlie spent part of the day giving the Hudson a thorough wash and clean. It looked quite smart again by the time he had finished, despite his task continuing into the heat of the day. The travelling party stayed another freezing cold night in Alice Springs, even water in Mr Murray's billy was partly frozen, a complete contrast to the hot day.

—

A day excursion to Temple Bar Gap was scheduled for Monday July 14, but first the party had to report to local police and let them know of their intended route. The policeman in Alice Springs at the time was Sergeant Lovegrove, who was responsible for territory that covered 236,000 square miles. Another local policeman was Constable Turnbull. A picnic lunch was packed in the Hudson

The stretch of water at Alice Springs isn't actually a spring but a body of water sitting in a basalt basin alongside the Telegraph Station.

and the four tourists climbed aboard for their excursion. The countryside was very pretty with sweeping, heavily timbered ranges attracting their attention. After lunch they headed to Heavitree Gap via the back of the range where they came across a mass of dead animals around a water hole. Continuing on through another gap, they sighted an inspiring flock of black cockatoos and stopped for afternoon tea under a shady tree in a dry creek bed. This also gave Ada the chance to seek some gemstones while Lil looked for flowers and Eileen admired the birds.

After a relaxing day-long tour Charlie turned the Hudson back toward Alice Springs where they called at the post office for mail, but there was little to be received. The evening was spent talking about the day's activities and writing letters to friends and family back home. Charlie's note to his son, Mervyn, expressed his desire to be at home with Hazel and the children, but he had a job to do and it would be several weeks before he could be with them again. The note read, "Hello Boy, I hope you are looking after your mother and sisters. All is well in Alice Springs", signed Dad. Mervyn was often referred to as boy, being the only one in a family of girls.

—

After all the travelling and the previous day's excursion it was finally time for a day off and a chance to catch up on some rest. Everybody spent the morning enjoying the glorious sunshine on the front verandah until Father Long arrived with an offer to show the visitors over his church that was built in one short year by volunteers. Prized amongst its fittings was a tabernacle door that was made from gold and studded with gemstones, all found in and around the Alice Springs region.

Being the oldest of the group, Miss Beal spent the afternoon resting, as did Charlie, but Lil and Eileen took advantage of an opportunity to visit Adelaide House, the local hospital, where they were given a guided tour by Sister Inglis and Sister Cavanagh.

Here they were shown the unique cooling system built into the hospital to counter the intense heat experienced in Central Australia in the summer. The Flying Doctor Service founder John Flynn, played a major part in the design and supervision of construction of Adelaide House which was built by Jack Williams, using local stone and timber carted up from Oodnadatta on camels in 1926. Flynn's design for the building included a cellar and a lantern style roof section that rose above the main roof. This allowed hot air to escape by natural ventilation, in much the same manner as a kerosene lantern. On hot days the nurses would shut all the windows and doors. Warm air would then escape from the top of the building and natural convection would draw cooler air in from the cellar to the various rooms. To enable this to happen there was a system of air ducts from the cellar leading to ventilators in each room. Wet, hessian bags were hung in the cellar to ensure the air coming through them was cool and free of dust.

A small hut at the rear of the house was the radio hut, where the first transmission from inland Australia was made by Alfred Traeger, also in 1926.

More postcard and letter writing filled the evening for the women, along with a hand or two of cards, but Charlie was content to get plenty of rest in preparation for more long days on the track.

It was more of the same for the next day apart from a shopping trip to stock up the larder and fill the petrol tanks for the next stage of the trip.

There was quite a bit of activity around the small township at this time as there was an expedition being set up to attempt to find the fabled "Lasseter's Reef". Harold Bell Lasseter claimed he had found the rich gold bearing reef in 1899, but several attempts to locate it again since that time had failed. In 1916 the WA Government sent a camel expedition to try to locate the reef, but there were too many casualties from attacks by the natives so it was forced to return.

On reading about these attacks only 14 years earlier, the ladies were a little apprehensive about continuing on to Darwin through even more inhospitable country, but with encouragement from the policeman and Charlie they decided to continue.

Lasseter was a friend of John Bailey, president of the Australian Workers Union in Sydney. He raised £5000 to form a company called Central Australian Gold Exploration Coy Ltd and the expedition was assembled in Alice Springs to search for Lasseter's Reef at the same time as Charlie and his passengers were passing through. The expedition used a six wheeled Thornycroft truck, designed especially for trackless desert exploration and provided free of charge by the Thornycroft company in England, as Britain's contribution to the attempt. Major de Havilland's plane, the Black Hawk II, was purchased and renamed the Golden Quest. The plane was to be used to keep the ground party in touch with civilisation and to search ahead of the party, locating water and a route for the truck. Atlantic Oil Union also donated 600 gallons of petrol and the State Government granted free transport for the truck, stores and men of the ground party. A second truck was also engaged in Alice Springs with Fred Colson, a cheerful Aussie bushman, with a reputation for initiative and resource as a driver.

The prospecting party chosen were; Fred Blakeley, leader; Harry Lasseter, guide; George Sutherland, prospector and miner; Phillip Taylor, engineer; Captain Blakiston-Houston, explorer; and EH Coote, pilot. Fred Colson also lent his Chevrolet car to the expedition so it could be used to bring Captain Houston back from Ilbilba, as he was due to return to duty.

Along with the 600 gallons of petrol, a hundred gallons of water and two tons of provisions and equipment were loaded. Colson's Chevrolet car carried another two tons of petrol. All Alice Springs turned out to give the cavalcade a rousing farewell as they departed on July 23, 1930, just a few days after Charlie Heard and his tourists visited the town.

Thursday July 17 was departure day from Alice Springs for the tourists, but not before calling by the post office to post mail and leave forwarding addresses. With that out of the way Alice Springs slowly disappeared behind the Hudson as Charlie pointed its bonnet to the north at 9:00 am. Just north of Alice Springs, they crossed Charles Creek that runs through a natural amphitheatre, a popular camping spot for travellers. The early going was quite rough, but after covering a dozen miles, the road smoothed out to near perfect condition and the party was

The Telegraph Station and its cluster of buildings was nearby, but separate from the town of Stuart, as Alice Springs was known, until the whole township area was proclaimed "Alice Springs".

confident of making it to Barrow Creek, halfway to Tennant Creek from The Alice, by nightfall.

Further to the north of Alice Springs there were government wells for 300 miles, spaced 20 to 30 miles apart. Each one had wind-laces and buckets, a large holding tank and troughs for animals. These wells were known as Burt's Well, Connor's Well, Ryan's Well and Ti-Tree Well.

Burts Plain, north of Alice Springs is 200 metres higher above sea level but the countryside returns to the same height as Alice Springs at Ti-Tree Well, where camels were used to "whip" water from the well. The first termite nests appeared on Burts Plain, but work crews regularly knocked the ant hills down so travellers could get through.

Flowers and birds attracted the ladies' attention through the middle of the day, but by early afternoon it became very dusty and warm, so Charlie kept the Hudson rattling along past Central Mt Stuart without stopping. This area was a favourite camp for the bullockies travelling south with their giant herds. John McDouall Stuart originally named this feature after his mentor Charles Sturt, as Central Mount Sturt, but it was later changed by the government, in recognition of Stuart's own contribution to inland exploration. It is very close to what was considered to be the geographical centre of the continent, a further tribute to Stuart's navigational skills.

There was only one room available at Barrow Creek, where the Overland Telegraph Station was run by Mr Claude Chapman with linesman Mr Fred Harris. When the Telegraph Station was established in 1874 the natives attacked it and two of the operators, James Stapleton, the Station Master, and John Franks a linesman, were killed. They are buried nearby.

Carting stores from Birdum to Newcastle Waters.

The one room at the recently opened hotel was deemed unsuitable, and there were some shady looking characters around, so Charlie elected to drive on a few more miles and set up camp in what turned out to be a dusty, prickly site. In the course of setting up the camp Ada disturbed the prickles and they were scattered all through her skirt which she had to change. Making matters worse was an unfortunate incident when Lil had a bad fall over the tucker box. It was not a happy camp and it was destined to get worse still.

The dusty day's travel had seen 175 miles pass under the tyres of the Hudson, but it had also left all passengers caked in fine dirt that proved troublesome to remove from clothes and skin. However, some solid scrubbing with soap and water from the nearby well had everyone feeling a little better by bed time.

During that night a strong wind blew up and caused almost incessant dust storms, making sleeping most uncomfortable. Adding to the lack of sleep was the fact that they had camped too close to the well. Consequently, the rattle and clank of hobbled horses and stock moving in and out to drink ensured that everyone spent more time awake than asleep. Maybe that one room at Barrow Creek wouldn't have been so bad after all.

—

Not only was it difficult to sleep in the uncomfortable conditions of the camp, it turned very chilly in the morning so Charlie was up and getting a quick breakfast ready by 6.45 am. Ada was still complaining about the prickles in her skirt and was keen to replace it at first opportunity to buy another.

The track winds its way through heavy sand north of Barrow Creek to Attack Creek, where John McDouall Stuart had an unfortunate confrontation with the Warumungu Aborigines, on one of his exploration expeditions in 1860. Stuart was the first white man to venture so far into this part of the interior and he was constantly coming into contact with the local tribes. Usually these meetings were amicable, if somewhat tentative, and the Aboriginals were often the saviours of such early explorers when they ran out of water and food. However, there were sometimes misunderstandings due to lack of knowledge of each other's cultures and that seems to have been the case when Attack Creek gained its name.

The Aborigines had brought cooked food to Stuart's camp that he and his companions Head and Kekwick understood to be gifts. However with the passage of time and the expansion of white man's knowledge of Aboriginal culture, it is now clear that the Warumungu were in fact offering a trade – food and water for some of the white explorer's magical utensils. When they attempted to remove such items from the camp Stuart believed they were just thieving so and so's and ran them out of the camp.

Stuart was anxious to get moving again as he suspected there would be trouble with the Wurumungu and he was correct. They soon came back and attacked his group with some ferocity, throwing spears and boomerangs and forcing them to turn to their rifles to fight their way through to open country. The Aborigines were just as anxious to redeem their pride and subsequently set fire to the surrounding countryside in an endeavour to trap the white party. It almost succeeded too, Stuart and his cohorts were very lucky to escape alive and they all recorded the attack in their diaries.

On reaching Attack Creek, Charlie and his car load of ladies pulled over at the well to have a chat to one of the locals. He turned out to be the owner of nearby Singleton Station who greeted them with an offer of lunch back at the station. Over lunch he regaled the group with his tales of venturing into the outback country in his early days, while the visitors admired the bean wood and iron wood trees in the garden, along with dozens of Zebra finches.

"I'm 'im," the station owner would say, as he referred to himself at the end of every sentence, relating all his tales of bravado as they ate.

After lunch, the travellers thanked their host for his hospitality and climbed aboard the Hudson once more. As soon as they were out of earshot they started laughing and mimicking the station owner and his peculiar "I'm 'im" catch cry.

"You know that bloke who accepted the taxi fare from three women to take them to Darwin and back?" ventured Charlie in a questioning tone. "Well, I'm 'im," he mockingly added, creating more laughter all round.

From 1:30 pm until 4:00 pm the Hudson hurtled along without stopping, apart from a brief look around the Devils Marbles boulder formations. A dry creek was reached and, since it was a suitable site to set up camp for the night, the decision was made to call it an early day. There were

After days of travel this bore came into view, but the water was salty. When you need water out here there is no choice.

lots of birds in the vicinity, always a delight to Miss Beal who noted two redback kingfishers amongst their numbers.

Miss Beal played her gramophone for the group, and any nocturnal fauna that happened to be around the camp, while letter writing to friends and family at home was the main focus until turning in for bed early. It had been a good day with 98 miles rolling under the wheels of the Hudson.

"Good-night from I'm 'im," chortled Charlie as they all bedded down for the night.

—

An early start next morning soon brought the travelling party into contact with a gang of Aboriginal road workers busily repairing the road. They were overseen by a jolly white man who had the crew working diligently.

Along the track today they passed Wycliffe Well, which had poor water and a new well was sunk here in 1937. Bonney Well and Kelly Well passed by later in the morning and Tennant Creek soon loomed on the horizon, where Mr Woodroffe, who ran the Telegraph Station with Mr Martin, invited them all to lunch. He had a superb garden and offered Miss Beal seeds from a wonderful Stuart's bean tree and replenished some of their supplies while they were enjoying his catering. Stuart's bean tree grows to a height of 40 feet and has a trunk diameter of two feet. The long pods shed bright scarlet beans that lie about the base. The aborigines used these to make necklaces. They are bitter to taste and have no commercial use, but they are attractive. The wood of the Bean tree

Thirteen hundred head of cattle in the desert near Alice Springs.

is very light, somewhat like Balsa. Ada later planted these bean tree seeds and successfully grew them in her own garden back at Lorne.

The countryside was getting better with each mile as they travelled north and roaming cattle became more prevalent. During the day the Hudson passengers noticed what appeared to be a shimmer on the horizon ahead that turned out to be a huge herd of cattle, heading for the markets in Adelaide. There were 1300 head in this huge herd, but that was typical for the drovers of the day who were charged with getting their valuable stock to market as quickly as possible.

Timing was everything for the seasoned drovers who undertook this mighty task. Leave too early and you would get stuck in the not-yet-finished wet season of the north, leave too late and the cattle would starve or die of thirst before the destination was reached. Early literature on the drovers is littered with tales of those who got it wrong, whether from their own miscalculations, or from natural disasters, and many of them perished in the process. Succeed and the reward was great and so the tales of the greatest drovers of inland Australia became the stuff of legends.

Through this area the drovers also encountered Gastrolobium (Deadly Nightshade) which has decorative flower like the sweet pea, but it is extremely toxic to animals – one leaf can kill a camel if it eats from the plant and it is also dangerous to sheep.

All along the route Miss Beal made a point of having Charlie stop the car so they could have a yarn to the likes of the cattle drovers. This was all part of her great adventure to the north and back and she was determined to see and experience as much of it as possible. The stories told by the outback people were just as important as the landscape and the very adventure of making the trip itself.

Banka Banka was for quite some time the most remote station in the outback, the last stepping off point from civilisation whether you approached from the north or the south.

A sandy patch on the road interrupted proceedings during the afternoon and Charlie had to resort to the coconut matting once more, the first time since leaving the Finke River district to the south of Alice Springs. The delay was minor and soon the Hudson was pulling into the homestead yard at Banka Banka Station, owned by the Ambrose brothers. One was away in Alice Springs herding cattle but the other offered the tourists a warm welcome.

Banka Banka was, for quite some time, the most remote station in the outback, the last stepping off point from civilisation whether you approached from the north or the south. It was established by Tom Nugent, the leader of a bunch of rascals known as the "Ragged Thirteen" who ganged together to travel to the Ord River gold rush. Nugent was also a noted Brumby buster and a great bushman, skills that would serve him well for the rest of his life. Several gang members of the "Ragged Thirteen" stayed in Central Australia where they established themselves in more legitimate pursuits. The "Ragged Thirteen" was a gang of desperados from South Australia and Queensland who essentially plundered their way to the Ord River goldfields by deceiving and robbing everyone along the way to get food and supplies. They duffed cattle, stole meat from butchers' hooks and raided the stores of unsuspecting station managers. As they progressed to the goldfields they shared their plunder with others on the road so they were never "dobbed in" to the authorities.

When the gold rush waned, Nugent rode the 1000 miles back to Tennant Creek where he became the Overland Telegraph linesman. While carrying out these duties he stumbled on the "nice little pocket of country" that became Banka Banka Station, eventually covering 2000 square miles.

Native companions were prevalent through this section of the trip, four of them congregating for this picture, taken by Charlie Heard.

Tom Nugent wasn't yet completely free of his duffing days, he stocked Banka Banka from poddy calves left behind by drovers on the move and scoured the valleys and surrounding countryside for unbranded stock that he conveniently rounded up, branded and moved onto his leasehold. Nugent built a simple log hut by a never failing spring at Banka Banka (Warramungu word for "many bees") and furnished it with only the very basics – a box, a form and a table. The walls he decorated with newspaper cut-outs of prizefighters and jockeys and pictures of Banjo Paterson held pride of place. As time went by, Tom Nugent became a pioneer of the great north road.

For 30 years Tom Nugent worked almost as a lone hand developing the property and upon his death left Banka Banka to his sister, whom he hadn't seen for 30 years. Her sons were the Ambrose brothers, Paddy and Arthur, a fine pair of stockmen who continued the family business for another 30 years, earning a great deal of respect in the cattle industry during that time.

Another member of the "Ragged Thirteen" was Jim Woodroffe. After the rush he returned to Alice Springs where he made a living initially by selling meteorites to museums. Perhaps the Mr Woodroffe of Tennant Creek who had offered Charlie and his passengers such fine hospitality was one of his descendants.

The accumulated dust from the sandy section of track negotiated earlier in the afternoon was washed off tired bodies and all enjoyed a sumptuous dinner cooked by the host and a friend who was also staying at the station. The hosts provided some musical entertainment for the evening and Miss Beal produced her gramophone to add to the evening's pleasure until late into the night. A green hide stretcher on the verandah of a nearby cottage became Charlie's bed for the night. He

More native companions, this time a larger flock watching the passing car with suspicion.

actually didn't mind, preferring to sleep outside when possible with the moon and stars for company and giving himself time alone to think about the family back at home.

—

Mr Ambrose insisted on cooking breakfast for the whole party before they climbed aboard the Hudson and waved goodbye at 9:00 am. One of the highlights of this morning's travel was an opportunity to stop and photograph a camel train being loaded by Aborigines and Afghans under the supervision of one white man. There were 41 camels in the train, all grunting, groaning and wheezing as they were loaded. Miss Beal later learned that the camel train supervisor was actually the person responsible for discovering wolfram (tungsten) in this area.

Morning tea was taken at Helen Springs where Ada delivered a letter to Miss Elsie Bohning, whose family owned the station. Here they found out that Elsie actually wrote articles about her life on the station for newspapers under the name "Little Bush Mai". Elsie's writings were published in the Northern Territory Times between 1921 and 1932, about life in the Northern Territory. And what stories they must have been, as included in her repertoire was being the first, along with her mother, to drove a mob of cattle to the new rail head out of Alice Springs. Elsie also collected specimens (insects) for Mr Le Souf of the Sydney Zoo. She later married Fred Harris who ran McLaren Station.

Mr John Bohning, Elsie's father, purchased a Dodge tourer in Adelaide in 1929 and drove it back to Helen Springs Station in November of that year, so the novelty of owning a new car was still burning bright.

At the Helen Springs station there was a beautiful semi-tropical garden where custard apples grew profusely. The Bohnings were busy with cattle branding, so the travellers elected to stay and watch for a while before moving on to Powell Creek.

Powell Creek Overland Telegraph Station had permanent water and the manager, Mr Ward, had a staff of five in total.

"The Perfect Host", Mr Ward welcomed them with open arms as he had been forewarned of Charlie's approaching taxi as more and more people in the outback became aware of their expedition. The bush telegraph was buzzing with news of their progress. Mr Ward was keen to provide some entertainment and he produced several gramophone records, that he hoped they could all listen to in the evening.

"Do you have a gramophone to play them on?" asked Miss Beal quizzically.

"No, but you do," was his quick reply, I have been waiting for you for ages.

Thanks to his network of outback informants he knew that Ada was carrying a gramophone in the Hudson. After listening to several of Mr Ward's records, Miss Beal indicated that it was time they loaded up and continued on their way. "The Perfect Host" was very disappointed as he wanted them to stay overnight, but they were all keen to keep moving on to Newcastle Waters.

From Powells Creek to Newcastle Waters the track is covered with rocks, stones, gibbers, crab holes, steps, deep ruts, sand and creeks. The condition of the track, plus the series of stops, meant the total distance covered for the day was only 43 miles, but that was enough to see them safely into Newcastle Waters by 5:00 pm. One of the local policeman, Constable Reid greeted them warmly and, along with Mr and Mrs Jack Sargent who owned the wine shanty, endowed them with the finest hospitality in the unusual double storey corrugated iron police station. The "bush telegraph" was in full swing and many people had come into the settlement to see the the Hudson taxi and meet its occupants.

Another well-known policeman from this locality was Phil Muldoon who was also a very good blacksmith. Dr Cook was the only doctor in Northern Territory/Central Australia at this time and he was also a regular visitor to the area, especially since he had purchased a new Chevrolet car in August 1929.

Newcastle Waters was the unofficial post office and store for drovers and travellers. The water hole when full was 800 metres long and in 1930 the Government resumed one square mile at Newcastle Waters for a town site, based around the police station. Newcastle Waters Station is at the "crossroads of Australia" and covers 4500 square miles, all run by a single man, Mr Burkitt. North the track goes to Darwin, south to Alice Springs and Adelaide, east to Queensland and west to Western Australia via Wave Hill Station, one of the largest in the world.

Charlie, Lil and Eileen went for a walk around the area while Miss Beal and Mr Sargent spent some time in deep discussion about the viability of continuing their journey to Darwin. There were rumours of an unknown disease being rampant at Katherine, but Mr Sergeant revealed that these

So high was the Mitchell Grass that Charlie had to slow the Hudson to a crawl and Miss Glenny was obliged to clamber up onto the extra fuel tank in order to see where the track went.

reports were greatly exaggerated and that it was, in fact, quite safe to continue. The tents and matting wouldn't be required between Newcastle Waters and Darwin so Ada asked Mr Sargent if it would be alright to leave them in his care until they came back through on their return journey.

—

The previous evening had proved a most interesting time and spirits were high the next morning when the group pulled out of Newcastle Waters. At first the track was very rough across the Sturt Plain, a sandy desert terrain with rough creek crossings. The hooves of cattle herds had made it worse as the Hudson bounced its way across the Mitchell Grass plains. So high was the grass in places along the track that Charlie had to slow the Hudson to a crawl and Miss Glenny was obliged to clamber up onto the extra fuel tank in order to see where the track went next.

This same long, coarse grass had hampered John McDouall Stuart when he was nearing the achievement of his south to north continent crossing in the 1860s, eventually forcing him to make a detour to find a way around it. Mitchell Grass (*Astrebla*) is highly regarded for fattening cattle, but the grass is very high north of Newcastle Waters where it is often too rank even for cattle. The area is known as "sour country".

Government wells were now more frequently placed and a halt was called at Daly Waters Overland Telegraph Station to send telegrams home and enjoy some lunch in a shady spot. The Telegraph Station was located in a ramshackle building near the "Stuart Tree" and manned by Mr Ashton and Mr Grant.

Having dealt with the telegrams and finished off a picnic lunch it was off to Birdum where the new hotel didn't have a room available as it was as yet unfinished, so the overnight stop was spent in a boarding house. Miss Beal and Miss Glenny shared a room, Miss Wilmot slept outside, but it was even worse for Charlie as he had to sleep outside in a shelter that he shared with the hens. He couldn't even enjoy a smoke as the petrol was also stored in the shelter. The owner was most apologetic for their uncomfortable surrounds and for the poorly furbished bathroom that, in fact, seemed to be part of the new hotel next door.

Miss Beal, ever aware of the local fauna, noticed pygmy flying possums around the boarding house.

—

There wasn't much sleep to be had so everyone was up at dawn and under way again by 7:00 am on July 22. The countryside all around was very pretty in this area and the ladies were enthralled by different types of birds and unfamiliar trees and shrubs. After travelling about 30 miles the policeman from Mataranka made an appearance, he was on his way to Birdum to investigate an apparent "ruckus" that took place the previous evening. That was news to our intrepid travellers, they hadn't seen or heard any "ruckus", but the fact that they might have been involved tickled Ada's funny bone.

Crossing a creek near Darwin.

"What a woolly time we must have had last night," she said, after the policeman was out of earshot.

The further north the taxi riders ventured, the better the country and the local stock looked. Today there were horses, donkeys and cattle, all in superb condition, roaming contentedly.

One of the highlights of this day's travel was passing by the Elsey Station, the homestead that was the basis of the book "We Of The Never Never" by Mrs Aeneas Gunn, wife of the station owner. The homestead wasn't visible from the road, nor the grave of the Maluka (Aeneas Gunn).

Mataranka, which consisted of a railway station, two Chinese stores and a pub, all made from tin, came and went without a stop as the Hudson scooted along to Maramboy, all stony hills and tin mining, where there was just a short pause to find the police station. The nurse at the local hospital invited Charlie and the ladies to tea, but they were eager to move on to Katherine for the evening stop. They weren't keen to have to make camp in the open through this part of the country as crocodiles are encountered from here to the north.

By 5:00 pm the Hudson was slowing down for the Katherine River where the banks are 100 feet high at the crossing, so a cutting had been made for better access on the north side. There was only a single shower available for everyone to use at O'Shea's iron, steel and concrete hotel. It was still a welcome refresher after which the travellers adjourned to the lounge for the evening, writing letters and relaxing in the comfortable surrounds.

Crossing the Adelaide River in the Northern Territory, just below Darwin.

Recent floods had done a lot of damage along the rivers closer to Darwin. Here at Adelaide River, 400 miles south of Darwin the bridgeworks had been washed away.

Charlie's Hudson at rest underneath the railway bridge, just south of Darwin.

By now Charlie was beginning to yearn for the children at home and his beloved wife Hazel. He dreamed of holding them in his arms as he wrote his letter home, telling Hazel how much he missed her. He reminded young Mervyn that it was his duty to be "man of the house" and look after his mother and sisters until Charlie returned.

After finishing his letter to home Charlie noted the mileage for the day in his notebook (135). During the evening the group met Miss Bohning's sister from Helen Springs station.

—

First duty for the day, before leaving Katherine at 9:00 am, was to post the mail prepared by the group members the previous night. At lunch time Ada had an unfortunate accident when opening a can of sardines. The contents had gone off and when she punctured the can it spurted all over her dress. The smell was terrible, but it had to be endured until they reached Pine Creek, an old gold mining settlement from the 1870s to 1880s, later in the day. A Chinese washerwoman was located to wash the dress, but it wasn't entirely successful, the smell still quite evident despite the laundering.

This area of the Northern Territory is notorious for white ant problems, but the locals had learnt to cope with them by sitting all the hotel bed and furniture legs in cans of water. The ant hills

Darwin Pier indicated the party had reached their northern most point on their adventure through Central Australia.

sometimes look like wedding cakes or cathedrals with buttresses supporting the central core. Some were narrow and even aligned north and south, inhabited by so-called magnetic ants.

A young man in a blue shirt made a nuisance of himself after having imbibed rather too much and disturbed everyone throughout the night. This was unfortunate as Charlie wanted to be early to bed and early to rise in order to make it all the way through to Darwin the next day.

Even as it became more common for adventurous travellers to drive to Darwin, this last section from Katherine to Darwin was often done by train. Cars were loaded onto the train, known as "Leaping Lena", for this last stretch, as the track was often too rough for motor vehicles, especially straight after the wet season. Not for Charlie though, he was determined the Hudson would be driven all the way to Darwin.

—

July 24, 1930 was to be a very big day and everyone was up before dawn. Breakfast was prepared and eaten by gaslight. It was still dark when Charlie turned the Hudson's hood ornament toward Darwin. The outline of that hood ornament and the front of the car itself looked ghostly behind the glare of the headlights that were being used for the first time since leaving Victoria. Despite having been warned that the road was in poor condition it actually turned out to be much better than expected. The track from Katherine to Adelaide River runs almost all the way beside the railway line. Dozens of creek crossings were required, some still having trickling, burbling streams of water running in them, which was a treat for all on board after the dryness of the interior.

Lunch was taken at the galvanized iron Adelaide River Railway Refreshment House, still 82 miles south of Darwin. This establishment was operated by Mrs Carroll and the food was given the tick of approval by all four travellers. Devastating floods had roared through this area of the Northern Territory during the previous February and large concrete railway bridges were completely destroyed. Workmen were in the process of replacing them all with steel structures that would better stand up to the rushing water in the future.

Miss Beal was keen to call on a local orange and lemon orchard that was owned by a German chap who actually claimed he was Canadian, but his accent gave his heritage away. This fellow had built a concrete dam with assistance from two aborigines. He pumped water to irrigate his orchard and garden and he was the main supplier of fruit to Darwin, usually sending it up by train.

It was 6.30 pm by the time the settlement of Darwin emerged before the Hudson, causing some excitement inside the car as the realisation hit home that they had made it all the way to the top of Australia. Total mileage for the day was 179, making it one of the longest yet traversed in a single day. Parts of the road had turned out to be as rough as predicted, but overall Miss Beal thought this day's journey was most picturesque and interesting in the extreme, and she had thoroughly enjoyed every part of it. No doubt that feeling was influenced by the achievement of reaching Darwin at last.

Charlie directed the Hudson through town directly to the Post Office where their waiting mail was retrieved with a smile by the Post Master, even though it was well past closing time. Next stop was the Victoria Hotel where they were warmly welcomed by Mrs Gordon, the "Queen of Darwin", whose husband had unfortunately passed away only a few months earlier. She was somewhat surprised to see the group arrive so early. She had expected they would put their car on the train at Katherine and therefore wouldn't arrive until the next day.

"You're the first car to make it through this season," she exclaimed, "You will be the talk of the town tomorrow."

The reward for the travellers was a hot bath and a good dinner.

The ladies were quite chuffed that they had successfully traversed the outback and made it to Darwin. Charlie was particularly satisfied as the Hudson had made it all the way with minimum fuss, no punctures and only the broken spring requiring attention along the way.

Mrs Gordon was so impressed she took Miss Beal aside, rested her hand on her shoulder and said, "Miss Beal, if there is anything you want and it is available in Darwin, you shall have it. It's not every day that we have a visit from a taxi from down south, so you and your party shall be treated like royalty."

That brought quite a smile to Ada's face. "Darwin", she thought to herself, "We have actually made it to the top." Ada Beal and her companions slept contentedly that night.

■ Chapter

8

A Top End Welcome

Comfortable

beds, combined with the weariness from the long day's travel was a sure recipe for a long sleep-in for all four intrepid travellers on their first morning in Darwin. By the time Ada emerged and planned the activities for the day it was already past noon. Miss Beal had intended to call at the bank, only to find opening hours were from 10:00 am to 12:00 noon each day. Eileen and Lil were astir a little earlier than Miss Beal and they had already made a visit to the shops before Ada caught up with them. Charlie had been active since he rose and had already organised a boating expedition to the Quarantine Station for the afternoon. It was a beautiful smooth day on the harbour and the water was as blue as the azure sky above. The boat didn't actually stop at the Quarantine Station but the outing was still enjoyed immensely by the Southerners. It was only while they were out in the boat that Miss Beal noticed the mangroves along the shoreline, and she was surprised not to have noticed them earlier.

Back at the hotel, there were invitations from the secretary of the Victoria League for all of the visitors to attend a dance they were conducting that evening. The ladies accepted the invitation, but

Miss Glenny and Miss Wilmott on the beach at Darwin with a twin masted sailing ship in the background.

According to Charlie's photo album, this was a hotel at Darwin.

for Charlie it was to be a hot bath, a cooked meal and early to bed.

Miss Beal was most impressed with the venue. The building was beautifully decorated and the whole layout was eminently suited for the entertainment of all guests. Lil and Ada played bridge on the balcony with Mrs Wardell, the Resident's wife partnering Miss Beal and Mrs Finnis teaming up with Miss Wilmot. Meanwhile Miss Glenny enjoyed the dancing inside and later in the evening they all enjoyed a tasty supper on the ground floor.

Another surprise was in store for Miss Beal when she met a former resident of Lorne at the dance. She had been a Miss Buxton before marrying and moving to Darwin. The pair chatted on for ages, catching up on all the news of Lorne since Miss Buxton had left.

—

The long days of travel had certainly caught up with Charlie, he spent the next day mostly just resting his weary bones. It was the same prescription for Miss Beal, choosing to rest while Miss Glenny and Miss Wilmot went shopping once again in the morning. Even in 1930 the pearl trade was active in the Darwin area and a Japanese pearl dealer showed the ladies a collection of the precious gems that was valued at £150.

The whole group spent the afternoon relaxing and reading, but by evening all felt refreshed enough to enjoy a drive to the Eastern Beach to take in the beautiful sunset. Charlie was happy to spend the rest of the evening listening to the gramophone and relaxing, but for the ladies it was another night of dancing. Darwin was agreeing with them all after the long trek and they were all happy to enjoy it in their own particular way.

After two days in Darwin, Charlie and the ladies were obviously much recovered from their travelling ordeal and the activity level started to rise accordingly. Sunday morning was spent at the hotel where Mr Hobbler treated everyone to what he called "Presbyterian Syrup". A drive to Drip Stone Caves was the after lunch entertainment, where there was a pretty beach, but a decided lack of sea shells, much to Ada's disappointment. However, there were plenty of wonderful birds to provide some natural cheer for the visitors. Olga Armytage had made a cake for the travellers to carry with them to Darwin and it was laid on for afternoon tea at the beach. Some locals were fishing nearby and having quite a bit of success so they gave Miss Beal enough whiting to feed everybody.

Monday morning was shopping time again with the first stop being the Curio Shop where the owner was an invalid and confined to a bed that he had situated in the middle of the shop. Customers took their purchases to him if they had questions to ask, or to actually make the purchase. Next stop was the gardens where coconuts were picked and opened so the southern visitors could taste the milk. More shopping was enjoyed on the way home with a stop at the Eastern Shop where gifts were purchased for friends and family back home. There was so much to see that an early halt to browsing was necessary so Charlie could transport them back to the hotel in time for lunch.

Rapid Creek was the destination for the afternoon outing where some time was spent in conversation with a group of fellow tourists who were enjoying a picnic. They had been taking advantage of the excellent fishing as well and gave the visitors 15 whiting that they had caught at the mouth of the creek. These were taken back to the hotel where the "Queen of Darwin" had them prepared and cooked for her guests. Shell collecting was also much better here than on the Eastern Beach so the ladies gathered quite a few to take home.

Once again it was time to enjoy music from the gramophone on the balcony in the evening. These few days in Darwin were turning into quite the holiday for Charlie and his fare paying ladies.

—

Tuesday morning was spent finishing the browsing and shopping in the Eastern Shop that had been interrupted the previous day. Mr Currie from the bank came by and escorted Charlie and the ladies through the bank offices and living quarters before taking them for a drive to the golf links. Here he was able to show them where Sir Ross Smith's first flight from England had landed. JM Bennett and WH Shiers accompanied Smith on that flight. Mr Currie also mentioned that he was among the first to greet Amy Johnson on her arrival just a few months earlier. She was the first woman to fly solo from the United Kingdom to Darwin in the period May 5 to May 24, 1930, shortly before Charlie Heard's Hudson made it to the northern township. She landed at the Fanny Bay Racecourse. Amy Johnson later died doing what she loved most when she crashed her plane into the Thames Estuary in London on January 5, 1941.

From there it was on to the botanical gardens where Miss Beal was surprised to find a pink Bougainvillea, the first she had ever seen. Afternoon tea was taken at a Chinese café after which there was a visit to Mendell's Beach to watch another amazing Darwin sunset.

The ladies enjoyed more of Mr Currie's hospitality in the evening as he escorted them to the pictures. Supper afterwards was back at the Chinese café, where Miss Glenny enjoyed a taste of "long soup".

—

More touring around the sights of Darwin was scheduled for Wednesday morning, the 41st day since they had left Lorne. Charlie drove to the front beach and the ladies visited the Curio Shop once more to purchase some native baskets that had been specially sent down from the compound for Miss Beal to inspect.

"These are quite exquisite," she remarked, and promptly selected three to take home to Victoria. Perhaps it was fortunate that they had left the camping gear behind at Newcastle Waters as the extra space in the Hudson was now being filled with souvenirs.

Mr Currie acted as host again for a visit to a local Joss House where the ladies burnt some prayer sticks and listened to he and Mr Miller tell them of stories about the Chinese settlement in Darwin. The ladies admired many interesting items such as dragons heads and beautifully carved wooden boxes, while an elderly Chinese man told them of sailors who stole parts of the Joss' and consequently attracted much misfortune at sea.

The foreshore at Darwin.

While relaxing after their evening meal, Mr Miller invited Charlie and the ladies to a picnic the next day. Meanwhile, Miss Beal was measured for a khaki skirt to replace her prickle infested one that she had been wearing on the way up to Darwin. All attempts to remove the grass seeds from the old skirt had failed, so Ada decided the best course of action was to replace it altogether.

—

Having now spent several days enjoying the tourist attractions of Darwin, Charlie decided he would have a sleep-in on Thursday morning while the ladies went off picking flowers and picnicking with the Herberts at Koolpingah. Mrs Herbert was away from the home but her daughter invited the visitors to return for afternoon tea following their proposed visit to the nearby lagoon. This beautiful spot was covered with purple and white water lillies so all agreed it was the perfect spot for their picnic lunch.

The serendipity of the lagoon setting was sharply interrupted when a large snake emerged nearby, obviously disturbed by the unwelcome visitors.

"Stay still," barked Mr Miller as he grabbed a large stick and tried to kill the snake. At the same time the driver ran and fetched a gun from the car and quickly dispatched the snake to another life.

Unperturbed, at least externally, Miss Wimott, Miss Glenny and Mr Miller went for a walk around the lagoon after lunch, no doubt keeping a wary eye out for more slithering reptiles along the way. Mr Currie stayed with Miss Beal by the vehicles and spent his time productively picking a bunch of beautiful blue orchids that he duly presented to Miss Beal.

The driver was apparently enthused with his shooting expertise and put it to further use, bringing down a green pygmy goose. More wildlife appeared in the form of a dingo that Mr Miller took a shot at, but it escaped unharmed.

Shooting implements were eventually stowed back in the car and the trip back to the Herbert's home for afternoon tea was soon under way. By now Mrs Herbert was home and she was dismayed that her visitors hadn't picked any lillies, so she sent the Aborigines to rectify the situation. Such was their generous stalks that they only just fitted into a kerosene tin, commandeered to accommodate them for the trip back to Darwin.

The picnic day was so enjoyable that the ladies were too late returning to the hotel for the evening meal so they adjourned to the Chinese café where Charlie joined them to eat. He had spent the day tinkering with the Hudson and tuning it up generally in anticipation of making a start on their return journey. In the evening everyone turned their attention to letter writing on the balcony of the hotel. There were so many interesting stories to relate to friends and family back home.

—

Friday August 1 was to be the last day in Darwin for the Southern tourists. Miss Beal picked up her new skirt which she found had been very well made. Then it was off to the banks and to spend a little more time shopping at Jolly and Co's store in Smith Street, in preparation for the trip home. Mr Wolf took Eileen, Lil and Charlie for a drive in the afternoon to visit the hospital and gardens. He also took photos of them by the memorial erected to commemorate Sir Ross Smith's flight from England. Meanwhile Miss Beal spent the time packing for tomorrow's trip.

In the evening everyone adjourned to the railway station to watch the arrival of the train from Birdum as there was a special party on board that had been arranged by the Pioneer Tourist Company. Charlie and his passengers were included in this special occasion due to their now recognised amazing feat of travelling all the way through the centre of Australia by taxi.

The final night in Darwin was once again spent on the balcony of the hotel enjoying pleasant conversation with Mrs Gordon and thanking her for her perfect hospitality. The "Queen of Darwin" had enjoyed their company as well, and she continued to do the same for scores of Darwin visitors until the family sold the Victoria Hotel in 1946.

■ Chapter
9

Farewell to Darwin

The days of taking in Darwin's sights and sounds had drawn to a close. They had been extremely enjoyable, but now it was time to turn and head for home. Everyone was up and about early on Saturday August 2 in order to get packed up, take an early breakfast and head off for Adelaide River. There was quite a crowd on hand to see the travellers off on their return trip, including Mr Hobbler, Mr Cousins, Mr Wolf and the bubbly Mrs Gordon.

Eight miles from Darwin and a couple of miles to the east of the Katherine track they came across the renowned magnetic ant hills where they paused to take some photographs. Most of these ant hills were later smashed during the World War II re-alignment of the north/south road.

Soon they were back on the road to Adelaide River. This road was in very good condition, so the Hudson was roaring along at a respectable pace when Miss Beal suddenly exclaimed "Oh, no, we've done it again. The pearl shells given to us by Mr Currie are still at the hotel!"

It was too late to turn back as they were closer to Adelaide River than Darwin and the steady pace meant they arrived by 12.30 pm, in time for lunch. A phone call to Mrs Gordon resolved the situation as she promised to send them on by post and in fact they actually beat the travellers back to Victoria.

It had been a beautiful morning for travelling and quite cool by Northern Territory standards. The scenery was quite different to what they had seen on the way up through Central Australia, much prettier and a very pleasant change from the sand, dry creek beds and salt bush. At one point Miss Beal had the opportunity to photograph a bower bird's nest that was completely surrounded with shells even though it was more than 75 miles inland.

In the afternoon a visit was made to the garden owned by the German fellow who was so insistent that they stay on the way up. He insisted on calling Miss Beal "Mumma" and Charlie "Puppa", much to amusement of all party members. Miss Beal purchased fresh lemons, mandarins and custard apples to eat along the way.

The drastic washaway at the railway bridge provided the opportunity for more photographs for the albums while crossing the river, but their peaceful picture taking was suddenly interrupted by the sound of a rapidly approaching car. A brief conversation with the driver as he crossed the river revealed he was on a dash to Newcastle Waters to purchase special fuel and oil for Mr Willie Oliver's plane in Darwin.

Despite having reached Adelaide Waters early in the day, it was decided to make it the overnight stop and this gave Charlie an opportunity to write a long letter home to his dearest Hazel. He was still a long way from home, but at least the Hudson was now heading south once more, every day bringing him closer to home and the family he was missing so much. The ladies also took this opportunity to write letters home, telling everyone of their fabulous holiday in Darwin.

The travellers came upon a Mr Pierce during the morning with a crew of Aborigines perched on his truck together with all the equipment necessary to cut pine trees.

—

By 8:00 am the next morning the Hudson was ticking over nicely as the passengers enjoyed a delightful drive to Pine Creek where lunch was taken at May Brown's hotel, at the exorbitant rate of 3/- each. Nobody was happy with the poor quality of the meal, especially at such an expensive price. They were relieved to hear that the annoying drunk lad in the blue shirt who had been so disruptive at this hotel on their way up to Darwin had since moved on, letting locals and visitors alike get back to life as normal.

After lunch, Charlie directed the Hudson toward Katherine, but a stop was made a few miles outside the town to camp for the night. It had been a good day of travelling with 134 miles covered. Everyone slept out in the open, Eileen and Lil on the ground and Miss Beal on the camp stretcher. The quiet surrounds amplified every little noise around the camp and Eileen claimed she heard a deer calling in the night. Charlie agreed it was quite likely in this part of the country, but no deer was seen.

Mosquitoes were very bad at this camp and nets were required before settling down for bed, but they were so annoying that Miss Beal and Miss Wilmot were awake again at 3:00 am and decided to drink their last bottle of ginger beer to provide a distraction. Miss Glenny was not impressed when she found out the next morning, she had slept through the night uninterrupted and missed out on her share of the ginger beer.

Everyone was up at dawn the next morning and breakfast was all over by 8:00 am. There was a sad farewell today as the deflated tyre was left behind. Inanimate object it might have seemed, but this tyre had travelled many miles in the Geelong and Lorne area on Charlie's Hudson and it had even been retreaded. After doing such sterling duty and performing all the way to Darwin it was like leaving a family member behind, but space was still at a premium, especially after all the shopping for souvenirs in Darwin, so anything that lightened the load a little was worth doing. Miss Beal spent a little time to say "goodbye" to the poor old tyre, and Chartlie even made a note in his diary about it.

Whenever fellow travellers were encountered along the road, Miss Beal liked to stop and share travelling stories with them. It was all part of that new experience she yearned for when planning this trip right from the beginning. So it was that they came upon a Mr Pierce during the morning with a crew of Aborigines perched on his truck together with all the equipment necessary to cut pine trees. These were to be used to build a new hotel at Daly Waters. There were two boys, a Lubra and several children in the group, all excitedly talking in their own dialect to each other while Charlie and the ladies chatted with Mr Pierce.

Soon the Hudson was humming down the road again and the day's trip went without incident until after lunch. Somehow, Charlie made a wrong turn and it wasn't realised until they had travelled some 12 miles in the wrong direction. Once the correct road was reached the travellers were keen to get back onto schedule so there was no stop at Mataranka this time, they would have to keep going to reach Birdum for the night stop.

Through this area the track mostly followed the railway line that remained unfinished for many years when work was suspended due to lack of funding. The accommodation was taken at the same house as on the northern leg of the trip and everyone was glad to reach it by nightfall as they were all caked with a layer of dust. They hoped it would be a peaceful night this time, after getting rid of the dust, but the Northern Territory dirt only gave way to hordes of mosquitoes. The evening was given over to letter writing as the air mail was due to leave from Daly Waters the next day. Efforts to keep the mosquitoes at bay were moderately successful and everyone headed to bed early after a hectic day. A pleasant sleep was enjoyed by the whole party, certainly it was a lot better than when they stayed here the first time.

An early start at 7:00 am from Birdum and excellent road conditions made for a comfortable morning's travel with only one stop, for water at a government tank. Charlie filled the water tank on the running board of the Hudson and topped up the radiator before continuing on their way.

An interesting encounter on this day was meeting up with a heavily loaded dray being hauled along by a team of seventeen horses. Miss Beal's usual reaction to such situations was to strike up

An interesting encounter on this day was meeting up with a heavily loaded dray being hauled along by a team of seventeen horses.

a conversation with the teamster and it was soon revealed that the owner-driver of this dray was quite a personality. He was known as "Irish Mac" (Jock McCarthy) one of the characters from the book "We of the Never Never".

The good driving conditions meant an early arrival at Newcastle Waters where Jack Sargent and his wife received them with their renowned cheery kindness. Despite the early afternoon arrival the sturdy Hudson had carried them effortlessly over 132 miles for the day.

The hosts related some gruesome stories of the manners and customs of the Aborigines, but it didn't stop the visitors from undertaking a walk to the nearby Aborigine camp in the evening.

—

Another early start was made to take advantage of the good conditions on Thursday August 6, as Charlie was keen to cover some extra distance on this day. Newcastle Waters to Camooweal in Queensland is a distance of 700 km along the Barkly Tableland Track that passes over black soil. The track was mostly in good condition but some hidden depressions would test the springs for an unwary driver. It was a monotonous landscape for most of the way. Low, open woodland gave way to tussock grasses but the area was badly affected by drought in 1929. Wells were established every 25 miles with wind mills and earth dams which saved many a weary traveller that previously would have perished.

The excellent road conditions continued right through the day and there were many sightings

Good driving conditions meant an early arrival at Newcastle Waters where Jack Sargent and his wife received them with their renowned cheery kindness.

of kangaroos during the trip. Anthony's Lagoon was reached during the afternoon where Miss Beal offered one of her "Letters of Introduction" to the local constable, resulting in an invitation to afternoon tea. Charlie was oblivious to the contents of these "Letters of Introduction", but he was aware that they seemed to open doors for them along the way.

Anthony's Lagoon is located at the junction of the roads known as the "cross roads of Australia". From here you can head north to Borroboola, east to Burketown, south east to Brunette Downs, one of the finest properties in Australia, and Camooweal, and west to Newcastle Waters. Anthony's Lagoon was an outstation of Brunette Downs, but it did have a provisions store.

There was plenty of activity in the area with workmen making a tennis court out of the granular material from the nearby ant-hills. Miss Beal also noticed a near new Tiger Moth aeroplane tucked away in a shed. A young man from Melbourne was holidaying at the station and he was able to point out the unusual chairs on the verandah of the Police station, interesting to the travellers because they were fitted with anklets for restraining miscreant Aborigines from time to time.

The station was also home to a herd of 500 goats that were coming into the yards for milking, but they weren't the only animal life they encountered in this active area. Once back on the road the Hudson ploughed into a swarm of huge locusts, each one almost three inches long. The easy access to food also attracted flocks of hawks and eagles, all so fat they could barely take flight as the Hudson motored into their dining room.

After driving clear of the locusts the Hudson's passengers were soon marvelling at the explosions of green bursting before them as they hummed along the road. Budgerigars, hundreds of them in each flock, provided marvelous entertainment for the ladies and temporarily distracted Charlie from his driving duties.

By the time Charlie lifted his foot to bring the Hudson cruising to a stop at the Blue Bush Bore, where they were to pitch camp for the night, the odometer indicated they had covered 180 miles for the day, a grand effort. The second night camping in the open since leaving Darwin was enjoyed by all under a beautiful clear, moonlit sky, but sleep was often interrupted by the howling of dingoes and the incessant noise created by cattle moving about near the camp. Sometimes they would be in packs of 20 or more and Charlie would have to resort to firing a couple of shots to scare them away and to reassure the ladies that they were safe.

—

The camp was packed up early and the Hudson was soon motoring toward Brunette Downs Station where the first stop for the day was made. This is one of the largest stations in Australia at 10,000 square miles. Lots of old derelict equipment lay about the station including an old road train, derelict cars and a workshop. It also had a wireless station so telegrams could be sent by the travellers. Harry Redwood, another gang member of the "Ragged Thirteen" had built Brunette Downs Station after returning from the Ord River gold rush. Charlie brought out his camera to photograph the Aboriginal children at the station and purchases of bread and meat were made from the station store.

Aboriginal baby in the Northern Territory.

A family of Aborigines in the Northern Territory.

Next stop was Alexandria Station where Charlie needed water for the Hudson's radiator. Here the party learnt that the station was the largest in the world owned by one person, a Mr Lloyd. The property covered 14,000 square miles.

Ada spent some time trying to obtain more information from one of the station hands, a boring, languid man who answered her many queries with a disinterested "Yep" and "Nah", much to her inner frustration which she managed to contain. Once back in the taxi she was still frustrated with this layabout and commented to the others, "I even asked his name and do you know what he replied? 'Yep'". That brought a good laugh from her fellow travellers.

Continuing on their way Charlie and the ladies caught up with another touring party they had met in Darwin and that had left before them. They were stopped at Rankins' store. Charlie was well satisfied to have come upon this party as it proved they were making good time on this first leg of the journey back to Victoria.

All through the afternoon of August 7 the Hudson purred along through arid, uninteresting country, interrupted only by the need to open and close gates and to answer the call of nature. When that was necessary, gentleman Charlie would wander off in one direction while the ladies headed in another. A "coo-ee" would alert everyone that they could all head back to the car without embarrassment. Charlie kept the Hudson under constant progress until camp was made at 6:00 pm. All were looking forward to a good night's sleep, particularly after the disturbances of the previous night.

■ **Chapter**

10

Crossing Queensland

Another

significant milestone was reached on Friday August 8, the 50th day since Charlie and the women left Lorne. On this day they would be passing from the Northern Territory into Queensland on their way to Camooweal. They were on the road by 7.30 am, keeping up a steady gait across uninteresting plains with little sign of life until they reached the rabbit proof fence that runs along the Northern Territory/Queensland border near Camooweal.

"Why would you want to keep the rabbits in?" asked Lil. "It's not to keep them in", replied Charlie with hint of laughter, "It's to keep them out!" That caused some amusement for the ladies.

The Hudson rolled into Camooweal, located on the Georgina River, at 11:00 am. The township consisted of two wooden pubs, bare gibber streets and drought stricken desolation, but it did have an air service and it was the service depot for the Barkly Tableland, making it an important stop for drovers.

Immediately catching the attention of all on board the Hudson were the extremely dry conditions around Camooweal with the town area extensively strewn with iron stone pebbles. First stop in town was the post office to collect mail, followed by oil and petrol, plus other requirements for the next stage of the journey.

With all of the purchases in hand, bookings were made at the hotel for a night of relative comfort after the previous nights of camping in the open. Welcome baths were a high priority for all of the travellers, Ada having to wait until almost 9:00 pm for enough water to be heated for hers, and even then only enough for use in a washing tub.

A pressing invitation to join a bridge party was politely declined as there was letter writing to complete in order to make the plane that was due to leave in the morning.

—

Daylight saw the Hudson rolling out through the common gate of Camooweal, bound for Mt Isa, shortly after pausing to watch the mail plane rumble into the sky. Today's destination was to be the new mining town of Mt Isa where silver and lead were discovered by a Mr Campbell only seven years earlier. Prior to 1930 many outback motorists used the alternative route from Camooweal to Longreach without passing through Mt Isa, but Charlie and his passengers wanted to see this booming mining town that had recently sprung up in the desert.

A brief pause was made along the way to photograph a grave with a fence around it in the middle of the track. This was the last resting place of a man who died of thirst after his packhorses bolted while he was attempting to cross from Northern Territory to Queensland. The monument was erected by his sister, who went searching for him, only to find him dead on the track. All four

A brief pause was made along the way to photograph a grave with a fence around it in the middle of the track. It is the last resting place of a man who died of thirst after his packhorses bolted.

stood gazing at the grave for a few minutes, a grim reminder that water and good equipment is the key to survival out here.

Many creeks were crossed during the day and soon after they passed through Kennedy's Gap and the Paroo Creek they crossed the Leichhardt River and drove into Mt Isa. The Hudson covered the 130 mile trip effortlessly, leaving the party plenty of time to look around the township, made almost entirely of corrugated iron houses, apart from the more elaborate homes of the mine managers.

Despite the original discovery being made in 1923, it was only in the previous two years that most of the development of the township and mine had taken place. By 1930 Mt Isa boasted two hotels, the one chosen by Charlie and the ladies being declared "black" by local workers for some undisclosed reason. Perhaps they thought the hotel owner had too much influence over their lives as he also owned the ice works and the power generator that provided power for the hotel and the "talkies" picture show.

The black ban seemed to have little effect on the pictures, as the ladies discovered when they attended that night to see "Dr Fu Manchu". There weren't enough seats for the paying public, some sitting three across two seats to avoid having to stand. Charlie struck it lucky. He decided not to go to the talkies, but found he could watch the whole show from the balcony of the hotel for free, the "theatre" not having any roof to impede his view.

Plans were made to visit the mine the next morning before leaving Mt Isa. The huge mine itself was a mile from the town centre, but the smelting works were quite close to the back of the town area.

—

Following breakfast at the hotel, Charlie loaded the Hudson in preparation for their mine visit following which they would resume their journey. While leaving the hotel Miss Beal struck up a conversation with a most interesting gentleman who left her his business card. He had just discovered an oil field.

Everyone clambered aboard the Hudson and Charlie directed it out of town past the two hills that stand like sentinels to the gateway of the mine. Even though it was Sunday, Charlie and the ladies expected to be able to visit the mine and inspect it at close quarters, however on arrival they discovered they needed a permit for such activity, and the mine officials were away at the time. Nevertheless Charlie was able to locate a very interesting gentleman who had a full knowledge of the mine workings and layout, and he was happy to share his knowledge with them.

From this gentleman they learned that the mine was working to a depth of 400 feet, but that water was proving troublesome at these depths. While they were listening to these descriptions a team of miners came to the surface, obviously from these wet areas, to emerge straight into the heat of the day. It certainly looked like hot, tiresome work in the mine.

More information from the group's informant revealed that the mine was yielding four ounces of silver to the ton and twenty-five percent lead. British and American investors had provided much of the finance to establish the mine and there were 20 American miners working at the time, although they were about to leave as their contracts were completed.

Satisfied that they had gained plenty of information on the mining activities of Mt Isa by mid-afternoon, Charlie fired up the Hudson and headed out of town past the aerodrome and the racecourse. Sixty-seven miles later they arrived at the small town of Duchess, where camp was set up for the night. It had been an interesting day and a nice break from the monotonous scenery they had encountered so far on this leg of the journey.

—

Mt Isa silver and lead mine in Queensland.

Mt Isa smelting works.

Mt Isa silver and lead mine employed just shy of 1300 men.

Fifty-three days had elapsed since the party left Lorne in mid-June and now it was August 10. A casual start at 9:30 am and it was only a short drive to Malbon where the morning tea stop was called. Gates had to be opened and closed along the way and the travellers passed by a couple of small aerodromes on their way to Malbon. Morning tea was taken at the local hotel that was noted for its beautiful museum that caught the interest of all of the visitors. The late start and time spent enjoying the museum meant the Hudson rolled across the bridge over the Cloncurry River and into the town of Cloncurry itself a little later than anticipated and they were too late for a planned lunch at the hotel. The short time spent travelling on this day resulted in only 65 miles being recorded, but that meant some more time to have a look around the town. The shop next door to the hotel was able to supply some lunch so that was the first order of the stay and then it was back to the hotel for hot baths.

A shopping excursion saw Miss Beal surprise Charlie with an informative map of Queensland along with some newspapers to catch up on the news of the world since they had left Darwin.

"Now we won't get lost, will we Mr Heard?" "No Miss Beal."

Under his breath he was mumbling to himself, "It's a bit late now!" But he knew Ada's comment was all in jest. After being in close proximity to each other for nearly two months they were all starting to relax a little, for they had now become good friends and Charlie was no longer just a taxi driver.

Miss Beal was soon in conversation with a Mr White whom she found very interesting and she promised to later send him a copy of "We and the Baby" by Hector Macquarie. Last thing for the enjoyable day was to send telegrams home to the relatives of each passenger, including one to Miss Glenny's mother to wish her "Happy Birthday from the Overlanders".

—

After the relaxing Monday it was back onto a tighter schedule for Tuesday with an early start on the road to MacKinlay. The Hudson passed out through rocky bluffs, across numerous creeks and rivers and 75 miles later reached MacKinlay, where lunch was taken at the hotel. From there the road to Kynuna was quite straight and the trip uneventful so Charlie pressed on a little further after reaching the township, to a suitable spot where they pitched camp for the night.

Charlie was keen to show his expertise with the gun to provide a meal for the party, but Miss Glenny didn't want him to shoot any of the fine flock of turkeys that were hovering nearby, so she chased them away. Charlie's sharp shooting did bring down a galah, which he promptly cooked for all to enjoy. But there was little enjoyment to be had, the wretched bird proved to be quite tough to chew.

"Not quite as good as turkey," said Charlie, "It would have been more enjoyable to chew on the pot it was cooked in!"

The disappointment of the galah feast was soon forgotten, replaced by the humorous antics of Miss Glenny, who had the misfortune to have her camp chair collapse underneath her. At least the others thought it was amusing, Miss Glenny was not so impressed with the uncomfortable outcome and was obviously equally unimpressed with the shrieks of laughter all about her. Not being able to find adequate words to express her disgust, she remained speechless and frustrated.

Earlier in the evening, Miss Beal had been wandering about the camp area while Charlie and the others set up the camp. She found many attractive shrubs, one with a brilliant star-like flower with a black seed in the centre that looked just like a button, from which she managed to capture some seeds to grow back home.

—

Charlie and Ada were both up early the next morning and took the opportunity of taking photos all around the camp-site, even though the others were still in their beds. By 9:00 am the Hudson was on its way from Kynuna and the passengers endured a stretch of mostly uninteresting country until the lunch stop was reached. While the landscape was uninteresting other aspects of the day's travelling more than compensated. Charlie and the ladies saw more kangaroos on this day than any previous. Large flocks of native companions were also encountered, one consisting of more than 20 birds.

During the afternoon the passengers were all intrigued by a slowly moving vehicle that loomed on the horizon. As the Hudson drew closer the vehicle revealed itself to be a big old wagon, drawn by 27 horses and loaded to the hilt with bales of wool, in fact 66 of them. The driver explained that he was on the way to Winton where the load of wool was to be scoured. He wasn't expecting to reach Winton for another five days, despite having seven spare horses tagging along. He also explained that it was proving cheaper to take longer with the horse drawn wagon and a big load, than to use the more modern and faster trucks that could carry less. He had tried the trucks but reverted to wagon freight to haul the eleven ton load all at once. Charlie and the ladies spent some enjoyable time conversing with the wagon driver, but they were soon under way again in the comparative comfort of the Hudson.

Winton was reached by 4:30 pm with 95 miles having rolled beneath the Hudson's tyres for the day. Winton was settled in 1875 and was linked to Longreach by rail in 1928. Longreach had been linked to Rockhampton by rail since 1892. The outback travellers were slowly moving back into more settled areas. Winton was the centre of a vast sheep and cattle grazing area. Nearby Dagworth Station is where Banjo Paterson wrote "Waltzing Matilda" in 1895 and Qantas was established here in 1923, only later to move to Longreach. Winton had electric light and water laid on, plus six pubs, one of which was the Great Northern Hotel, the chosen venue for the evening's stay. Miss Beal enquired here after Mrs Knowles, only to find that she had left the week before. For the first time since leaving Darwin ten days earlier, the travellers were able to enjoy the comforts of "real" baths.

—

Slowly, ever slowly, the trundling Hudson was bringing Charlie and his fares closer to normal civilisation. From Winton they set forth early on August 14, turning right past the hospital and out onto the road to Longreach, their target for lunch and an overnight stay, so that they had some time

Kangaroos are disturbed by the Hudson passing nearby.

to inspect the local attractions. Twice on this leg of the journey they passed through gates in the rabbit proof fence. Such long distances already travelled meant all were acutely aware of the mileage indicator in the Hudson's dash and today it registered 4444 miles since leaving Lorne. Quite near the town a company was drilling for oil, but apparently water entering the bore was proving troublesome. There was a water bore nearby at Blythesdale from which the party could see the oil derrick in the distance.

Longreach is on the Thomson River that becomes Cooper Creek and their arrival had all the passengers marvelling at the street names, all called after birds. How appropriate then, for a magpie to join them at lunch in a friendly manner, as they are prone to, when morsels of food are on offer. This one made the replacement campfire tripod his temporary home while he was offered, and greedily accepted, pieces of meat.

For days on end Charlie had been "entertained" by the ladies singing operatic and classic songs, but Ada determined it was time for a change. She sought and purchased a hymn-book in Longreach and so they added holy harmonising to their repertoire from this point.

—

First chore for Charlie on Friday morning was to drive Miss Beal to the bank where the obliging manager, who was most interested in their escapade, arranged for their party to visit the wool scouring works at Ilfracombe. By 9:30 am the Hudson was purring its way out of Longreach and by the time they reached Ilfracombe later in the day, the forewarned manager of the works was expecting them. Each was offered a sample piece of the finest wool being sent off to England. More fascinating experiences awaited the party as the manager took them to their bore water supply point. Holding a match to the gushing bore the group was startled by a foot long flame erupting from the water as it was accompanied by natural gas as it flowed to the surface.

The near boiling water from the bore was a tremendous advantage for the scouring process, but the heating process needed to be supplemented a second time through the works' own boilers, that were fired, callously it seemed to the visitors, by beautiful logs of "Gidgee" wood. All were impressed by the Gidgee's circle of almost pure white wood, surrounding a central milk chocolate coloured core. Miss Beal likened it to Raspberry Myall, an acacia wood that smells like raspberry, and the manager informed them that it burned with a tremendous heat, easily the best wood in Queensland for this purpose.

Having thoroughly enjoyed their visit to the scouring works, the ladies joined Charlie in the Hudson once more and the big tourer was pointed toward Barcaldine for the lunch stop. The hotel manager at Barcaldine drove the group in his own car to the local water supply. Once again it consisted of a boiling hot bore that was pumped into a huge water tank mounted on tall steel poles and capable of holding 47,000 gallons.

Back at the hotel the proprietor showed the ladies her personal collection of birds and plants, mostly of a tropical nature. Silky Oak is common for building and furniture making in these parts of Queensland, but never had the visitors seen such quality as that used to make the staircase in the hotel. Charlie's passengers also viewed a variety of pretty plates at the hotel and purchased several as souvenirs to take home.

After lunching at the hotel it was back on the road once more, this time with Blackall as the final destination for the day. Here the proprietors of the hotel had also been forewarned of the impending arrival of these adventurous travellers, and to afford them the best rooms and services available. Now the outback adventurers were beginning to feel a little like celebrities, and they were, for their story was now preceding them on the return journey and people were coming out of homes and work places to greet them as they passed through townships. Nearly everyone knew about the ladies and their taxi driver, Charlie Heard. It had been a busy day, but still one where the Hudson had traversed 135 miles through the Queensland outback.

Charlie finished a rewarding day by sending a telegram home to Hazel with the latest news of their travels. Simple words, "Arrived Blackall all's well, miss you. Love Charlie."

The telegrams were always short and to the point like this, you paid by the word and a message of this length might cost a shilling or more when five or six shillings was a day's pay for many. Even though the messages were short, Charlie knew Hazel would cherish every telegram and she kept them all.

Ada and Lil spent the evening writing letters home, but Eileen was fortunate to spend her evening with some friends who lived at Blackall.

—

Soon after 9:00 am the Hudson rolled out of Blackall, where all the streets are named after flowers, and followed the Barcoo River to the south. The travellers came across two teams of 20 horses, each pulling massive loads of wool past the fascinating gateways that caught their attention since leaving Camooweal several days earlier. They appeared to be every size, shape and condition imaginable. All through this same area were the spectacular "bottle trees", especially in the streets of Tambo. Charlie likened their shape to that of a milk bottle, with foliage only at the very top. Lunch was taken in the bush under one of these odd-shaped trees and the stop for a meal also gave them the chance to closely inspect many strange trees, shrubs and flowers. Closer to Augethella stands of Cypress became evident, along with many more amazing gates, including one with a white obelisk alongside. The evening stop-over was planned for Augathella, but the Ellangowan Hotel was not to the liking of the ladies, so the stop was kept brief enough just to purchase some fresh supplies. Charlie drove the Hudson some six miles out of town where a lovely quiet place was found to pitch camp for the night.

It was a cold night so the evening meal was quickly prepared, allowing Lil and Eileen to hop into bed early, while Ada tended to the entertainment emanating from her faithful gramophone, until the cold became too much for her, despite being wrapped in a blanket. Hot coffee, courtesy of Charlie, was welcome to ward off the cold and then they too turned in for the night after Charlie noted down the 144 miles travelled for the day in his increasingly battered diary.

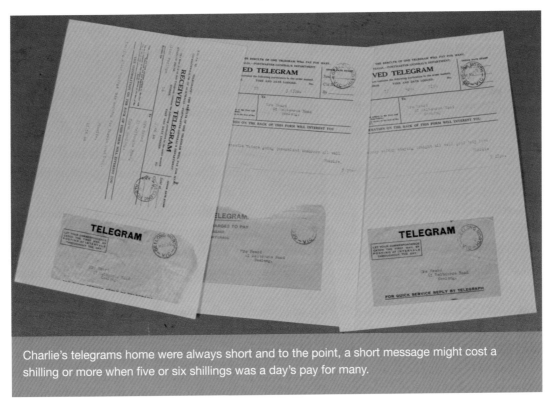

Charlie's telegrams home were always short and to the point, a short message might cost a shilling or more when five or six shillings was a day's pay for many.

By August 17 it was becoming apparent that the outback was slipping away behind the Hudson and increasingly civilisation was returning. A pair of almost tame butcher birds joined the party for breakfast, happily gobbling up every morsel offered to them by the ladies. Long avenues of trees along both sides of the road that morning were further evidence of the emergence from the desolate outback, as was the presence of the railway line right beside the road. At least 10 emus made it onto the list of wildlife recorded for the day. Each day the flora was becoming more varied and was the subject of fervent discussion over lunch at Morven and throughout the afternoon's drive to Mitchell, where rooms were taken up at the Hotel Richards.

An early finish to the day gave Charlie the chance to call into the Overland Garage and catch up on some maintenance on the Hudson. Grease nipples were all attended to and the front wheel bearings were packed with fresh grease at the same time. The ladies spent the evening attending to correspondence home while Charlie sent a telegram to Hazel, giving her a short description of their position and to let her know that all was going along well.

—

From Mitchell the roads became much better, but that was unusually disturbing for Charlie. The lack of road noise and undulations gave him the opportunity to identify some new and worrying sounds. A constant tickatickaticka sound filtered up to Charlie in the driver's seat from deep under the front of the Hudson.

"Wheel bearings", thought Charlie, "All those miles of plunging through the sand in Central Australia and the fording of creeks near Darwin must be taking their toll".

Morning tea was enjoyed in Roma, but soon it was back on the road again for the Victorians. A large truck was laid up on the side of the road so Charlie pulled the Hudson over to see if he could help. There was nothing he could do, as the truck needed new parts, so the travellers bid the unfortunate driver good-bye and good luck, and continued on their way.

Lunch was taken in the bush that day with Charlie performing his usual tea making duties while the ladies tended to the food. Ada opened cans of preserved meat and fruits and Lil and Eileen laid out the usual table – a box on the front seat. Charlie preferred to stand while eating his lunch, using the water tank on the running board as his table while the ladies enjoyed their lunch in a more civilised manner.

Charlie decided to investigate the front wheel bearings further, as they were now causing him some concern. There was little he could do apart from add more grease and hope that they would last until replacements could be obtained in one of the larger towns that were now within striking distance.

The rest of the day's travel was somewhat uncomfortable through avenues of prickly pear, until Miles was reached after dark. Rooms were taken at the hotel but the ladies were disappointed to find that there was no bath available, as that room had been converted into another bedroom. Sleep was hard to come by as other hotel patrons listened to the wireless broadcast of the cricket test match until the early hours of the morning. Ada was not impressed! She was so annoyed at the other patrons that she made no attempt to be quiet when she arose the next morning. In fact she was quite the opposite, much to the approval of the other ladies.

The road from Miles was better for the morning's travel to the dry Jinghi Jinghi Creek bed where the lunch stop was made. Extra entertainment was gained here by the antics of a magpie that flew back and forth from the impromptu feast to carry scraps of food to its young, high up in their nest above.

Charlie pressed on to Dalby with a view to purchasing a new tyre for the Hudson, but there was none to be had. The ladies were taken in by the beauty of the blooming wattles along the way, but they were scant distraction for Charlie, he was still hearing that ever ominous tickatickaticka from the wheel bearings. How much longer would they last?

All afternoon they kept company with the railway line to Oakey, where the road veered away from the railway line, then straightened for the last 20 miles into Toowoomba. By 5:30 pm the outskirts of Toowoomba loomed on the horizon and Charlie drove straight into the centre of town in order to locate the post office so that telegrams and letters could be sent home before it closed.

Having noted down 136 miles travelled for the day, Charlie joined the ladies for a pleasant evening meal at the Club Hotel where they were all staying. An after dinner walk saw them return with fresh fruit and an appetite for sleep.

—

Thick fog was encountered on the trip down the mountain out of Toowoomba, so the passengers in the Hudson were denied any views of the surrounding countryside. Poor road conditions made for very slow progress through Helidon, Grantham and Gatton, except for those few sections that were recently made. Charlie was very surprised at how bad the roads were, describing them as the worst encountered, quite a statement, considering where they had already been through the centre of the country. Mechanical problems started to emerge on encountering the bad roads and Charlie was anxious to get to Brisbane, where some repairs could be carried out. Some relief was gained just outside Ipswich where the road was sealed with bitumen and finally the Brisbane city loomed into view. The Hudson rolled into the Gresham Hotel for the first night's stay. Charlie described it as only being in fair condition, but it enabled them to unload and get the Hudson to the garage for some much needed work. Miss Beal and the ladies weren't impressed with the hotel at all, there was no sitting room and they decided they would move to a better establishment tomorrow.

Meanwhile it was telegram and mail checking time. There were a number of letters and parcels waiting at the post office, but one parcel had gone missing. It was located later, after endless correspondence with the PMG, it had apparently been taken by an A. Beal, described by Miss Beal as obviously being of doubtful character!

Another passenger was to join the group here in Brisbane and travel back to Sydney with them. Ada telephoned Alice in Sydney where she was staying with another friend Wynn, letting her know they had arrived in Brisbane. Alice caught the train to Brisbane the next day, leaving the harbour city at 3:30pm.

—

Next morning Miss Beal contacted her friend Mrs Howitson regarding a better place to stay. Her recommendation was to move to the Canberra Hotel which they would find much more comfortable – and cheaper. The Hudson spent its day convalescing in the garage, its mechanical ills being attended to in preparation for the last legs of the journey. Lil and Eileen spent part of the morning shopping and in the afternoon everything was packed up and moved to the Canberra Hotel where Eileen met a friend from Oriomo.

—

More shopping took place on Friday morning August 22 before the whole group were invited by Mrs Howitson for lunch at Rowe's where they were surprised to enjoy strawberries so early in the season. The afternoon was spent sightseeing, with visits to Highgate and One Tree Hill (Mt Cout-Tha), almost 1000 feet above the ocean. Low cloud restricted the views over the city somewhat, but all agreed Brisbane was indeed an exceedingly pretty place, being surrounded by hills with the river winding its way through the city.

Late in the day the whole group made their way to the railway station to meet Alice who arrived from Sydney on the 6:40pm train. It was a happy time for all with much excited talking by the ladies as they described their trip so far. Now Alice would experience some of this excitement as they prepared for the next sector of the journey with an extra passenger on board.

—

Touring around Brisbane continued on the 65th day since the travellers left Lorne and a visit to the Shell depot in Brisbane, after some early morning shopping, was one of the highlights for Charlie and the ladies today. Lunch was taken in a café in the city and was followed by a drive to Redcliffe, 14 miles north of Brisbane. Steady rain didn't deter the travellers who enjoyed a delicious feast of oysters, while the rain left glistening drops on all of the plants, giving them a welcome freshen up. Amongst the plant life that caught Ada's eye on this trip was the first bracken they had seen since leaving Victoria. Bamboo and brown berries were obtained along with some pretty mauve flowers. There was a brief stop at a roadside stall on the return trip where the ladies bought a selection of fresh fruit and then it was back to Brisbane for dinner. Charlie relaxed at the hotel for the evening while the four ladies went to the talkies to see the film "Atlantic" but they came home mumbling about the poor quality of the show.

"What a rotten show!" groaned Miss Beal, "It was so bad that Alice walked out at half time."

—

It was still raining when the loaded Hudson began its journey out of Brisbane, but they hadn't gone far when Charlie quickly became aware of a problem that urgently needed attention. Each time he put his foot on the brake pedal the rear brakes locked on and were reluctant to release. The Hudson would have to go back to the garage to find out what was wrong, so the ladies decided they would do some more sightseeing around Brisbane by local taxi, while Charlie attended to the repairs.

The gardens and surrounding suburbs were visited in the taxi and afternoon tea was taken at One Tree Hill (Mt Cout -Tha), the ladies' second visit to this landmark. Once again their view was hindered by persistent rain, but they did see a magnificent blue and grey budgerigar that Miss Beal described as "one of the loveliest birds imaginable".

Back at the garage Charlie had discovered a broken return spring in the rear brake of the Hudson, so he searched the garage for something similar and modified it to take the place of the original. But there was a further problem, a rear axle seal was leaking and that would take a little longer to repair. It was looking like yet another day would have to be spent in Brisbane.

In the evening the ladies headed off to the Cathedral, the interior of which impressed them mightily. They were also taken by the distinctive voice of the parson who led the evening service, although he was difficult to hear.

—

The extra delay provided the opportunity for the ladies to do some more local taxi touring, this time being taken on a shopping spree. A visit to the town hall tower gained an added dimension. When the tower clock struck 12:00 noon, the reverberations of the bells caused some alarm for the ladies because they were so close to them. They also learned of a recent occasion when the clock bells began chiming and couldn't be stopped, much to the chagrin of the local populace who telephoned the mayor and councillors incessantly through the night to get the din to cease! Despite the noisy location the view of the city was superb.

Charlie went along with the ladies after lunch as they visited the Shell Depot while the repairs continued on the Hudson. The manager showed the visiting party through the laboratory, the holding tanks and the supply outlets for the ships. Whilst touring the facility the group was introduced to an inventor, coincidentally named Mr Shell, who was responsible for the cleaning additive product known as Shelloc, only available in Queensland at that time. Mr Shell also invited the guests to join him for afternoon tea in the office. Then it was back to Mrs Howitson's for a second afternoon tea, a wonderful spread, but the host was surprised that they didn't eat more. The evening was spent packing again for another attempt at leaving the next day. Charlie wrote a letter home to Hazel, informing her that the Hudson was up and running once again.

Chapter
11

Southbound to Sydney

Charlie was keen to get everyone organised early the next morning

and into a car provided by the hotel to take them to the garage where the repaired Hudson awaited. By 9:00 am they were on their way again, this time successfully, and soon powering down the road to Beenleigh, where they paid the one shilling toll to cross the bridge and continued on to Southport. The road was in good condition, apart from a few sections that were still being worked on, but it was a relief for Charlie to have the Hudson humming along again. A short, 50 mile jaunt had them in Southport for lunch and the new passenger, Alice, was enjoying her introduction to a driving tour immensely.

Charlie described the hotel they stayed at as beautiful, while Miss Beal was taken with the parquetry floors, mostly made from Australian revillea. The ladies watched a man fossicking for oysters, the first time Ada had seen such a thing.

After lunch the tourists took a short trip to the ocean beach where they undertook a brief walk. Not finding many shells they soon opted for the relative comfort of the kiosk where they enjoyed afternoon tea and watched the birds from the verandah. The remainder of the afternoon was spent strolling around town and shopping for fruit to take along with them tomorrow for lunch.

—

It was 9:00 am on a beautiful sunny morning when Charlie turned the Hudson down the coast out of Southport toward Burleigh and Coolangatta, the border town that straddles the Queensland and NSW border with Tweed Heads. Everyone thought it was odd that there was a post office for each side of the town, only a quarter of a mile apart. The road to the border was in excellent condition, so it seemed like no time at all and they were loading onto the Chindera Ferry across the Tweed River. First stop was at a large sugar mill at Condong on the bank of the river, but staff members were too busy to provide an escorted tour. Nevertheless the tourists were left to their own resources in looking over the mill for about an hour. Samples of sugar cane and refined sugar were added to their souvenir kits and then it was on to Murwillumbah for morning tea. From there the route took the travellers to Mullumbimby for lunch, but then the condition of the road deteriorated quite considerably, slowing down progress and delaying their arrival into Casino until almost 6:00 pm. Still, there was time after dinner for a walk around the town and to take in more of the beautiful foliage and the many flame trees that were in bloom. It had been a productive day with 123 miles passing underneath the tyres of the Hudson.

Waiting for a bullock wagon to pass, NSW.

Carting timber by bullock wagon, NSW.

Travelling in each different state required a registration permit for motorists crossing the border so the first port of call on Thursday morning was to the police station in Casino.

"You should have obtained one at Tweed River", was the gruff response to Charlie's request for the permit, and so they continued on their way, unregistered for travel in NSW.

The permit episode was soon forgotten as the Hudson hummed along through very interesting countryside, with only a minor interruption at the Clarence River where another punt ride was required. Grafton was the lunch stop for this day where all enjoyed a serve of beautifully cooked fish. From here the road ventured into more mountainous terrain where the timber growth was very dense. A bullock team was soon encountered, all the passengers being taken by the great beasts straining hard to move a heavy load of huge logs up the hill.

Afternoon tea was taken in the bush by the roadside where the peace was destroyed by the ladies, all being struck with an uncontrollable fit of the giggles. Charlie wandered off into the bush mumbling to himself, "You would get more peace and quiet inside a galah's cage." Ada gathered some fern plants to send to a friend back home who was able to get them growing successfully. The day's journey ended at Coffs Harbour shortly after 5.00 pm where the party booked into a hotel that was described as being much improved over recent examples.

View of Nambucca Heads NSW.

The bullock wagon makes way for the Hudson to pass.

River crossing by punt, NSW.

View of the river, taken from the punt while crossing a river in NSW.

Waiting for the punt to reach the Hudson, waiting patiently on the river bank, NSW.

Around Coffs Harbour there are some fine beaches, so Miss Glenny and Miss Wilmot went surfing before breakfast, but they were still able to have breakfast and start down the road again by 9:00 am. Another ferry ride on the six car ferry was required at Raleigh where Charlie and the ladies crossed the Bellinger River. Morning tea at Nambucca Heads was the aim for the first section of the day's drive, once again through beautiful mountainous countryside. Here Miss Beal was taken by how similar Nambucca Heads was to her home-town of Lorne in Victoria. More bullock teams hauling giant loads of logs were encountered on the road between Nambucca Heads and Kempsey where their arrival coincided with lunch at the Royal Hotel.

No sooner was lunch completed than the Hudson was stirred into action once more with Port Macquarie the next town to be visited. A slight detour was required to visit Port Macquarie so Charlie turned the Hudson to the left as they came off the Blackman's Point Ferry over the Hastings River. In Port Macquarie Miss Beal was taken by the old St Thomas' Church of England, that was built by convicts in 1824. Having enjoyed the sights of the seaside town, Charlie once more directed the Hudson down the road to Taree where the stopover for the night was to be made at the Royal Hotel. They crossed the swing bridge at Coopernook and arrived at dusk. A short walk around town after their evening meal refreshed everyone before turning in for an early night. Friday had been another good day of travelling with 153 miles added to the Hudson's odometer.

—

The township of Gloucester NSW.

Gathering wild flowers in NSW on the way from Brisbane to Sydney.

The Tinonee Ferry over the Manning River was one of many punts and river crossings that were encountered on the morning run from Taree to Gloucester, where morning tea was taken. Here Charlie directed the Hudson into the bush so the ladies could see the prolific wildflowers in bloom. What a wonderful sight it was, with violets, orchids and a gorgeous, large yellow pea to capture their attention.

Charlie took photos of the ladies as they clambered down off a cutting beside the road and seconds later Lil slipped, tumbling to the ground below. She didn't hurt herself in any way, but her landing was somewhat undignified. Ever the gentleman, Charlie ran to enquire after her welfare, to which he received a curt, "No, only my pride as it was not very ladylike to end up like that." Charlie started to smile and suggested that maybe he should have waited a couple more seconds before taking the photo.

Soon Charlie had the Hudson back on the road toward Newcastle, but something wasn't right. The steering seemed to wander more than usual and Charlie had the distinct impression that the Hudson wasn't handling like it should. A stop was made to investigate and the problem was soon obvious, one tyre was going flat. The pump was brought into play, but with little impression being made, Charlie decided to wave down another driver for help.

Three young men on their way to a football match pulled their car to a stop at Charlie's beckoning and they were of great assistance in changing the wheel. Once again the only payment required was a tip of the hat and a firm handshake for the three boys and they were on their way

Lake Macquarie near Newcastle, NSW.

again. The flat tyre hadn't caused too much delay and soon the Hudson was behaving perfectly as they zipped along the road to Hexham, where another ferry ride was required to cross the Hunter River, before proceeding into Newcastle by 4:00 pm.

Charlie directed his attention to getting the tyre repaired, while the ladies hired a local car and toured the sights of the city, marvelling at the beaches and being surprised at how large the township of Newcastle had become.

Meanwhile Charlie discovered the reason for the deflating tyre, a faulty valve, that was soon rectified and the tyre refitted to the Hudson.

Miss Beal spent the early evening buying up a good supply of fresh fruit and later in the evening all of the ladies decided it was time for a night at the movies. Their popular choice was Maurice Chevalier in "The Big Pond". It brought an end to another very good day as the climate and surroundings returned to something with which they were all more familiar. Tomorrow Sydney beckoned.

—

The road out of Newcastle took the travellers south toward Belmont and it was a little unusual in that it was concrete for most of the way. From Belmont the road continued on to Swansea where the bridge crossing enabled the passengers to see right into Lake Macquarie and soon they were out into more beautiful wildflower country. From Wyong the road ran parallel with the railway line and

View of the Hawkesbury River.

A street scene as the group reached Sydney.

Having a spell on arrival in Sydney.

Miss Beal playing with friend, Wynn's dog in Sydney.

crossed it three times before they reached Gosford. Before long the Hudson passed by the old road to Wiseman's Ferry and soon the passengers all seemed to notice that the cars coming toward them were in groups of 28 vehicles. The reason soon became obvious when they reached Peates Ferry across the Hawkesbury River – it carried 28 cars at a time. The ferry crossing was interesting too, the punt floating a considerable distance downstream as it crossed. On landing they purchased some beautiful waratahs and native roses some of which Ada arranged to be sent on to Melbourne.

The first point of call in Sydney was to Miss Beal's friend Wynn, who lived in Hunters Hill where they were all warmly greeted. A celebratory lunch was enjoyed before moving on to Fig Tree, where Wynn had rented a flat for the travellers. Wynn and family followed along and they all enjoyed dinner together before Charlie and the ladies retired to bed, somewhat weary, but also relieved at having achieved so much of their intended journey with relatively few incidents. The Hudson was parked in the back yard where even it looked remarkably comfortable, considering the punishment it had endured over the past two and a half months.

—

Breakfast turned out to be somewhat of an ordeal as Ada couldn't get the gas to work and had even less success with the gas company. The only option was to eat breakfast out, at a nearby café. Charlie

The three ladies enjoy the botanical gardens in Sydney. Miss Beal standing, Miss Wilmot sitting at the left and Miss Glenny on the right.

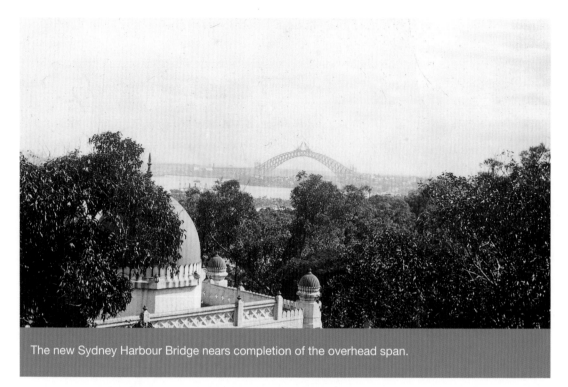
The new Sydney Harbour Bridge nears completion of the overhead span.

and the Hudson were both given a welcome break from the local tripping about that was planned, with the first call after breakfast being made to the post office in a taxi. From there the travellers were taken to the gardens where they spent the time reading their mail and waiting for Wynn, Alice and Marion who were to join them on their day-trip to Taronga Park Zoo.

Local taxis were used for this trip too, but it wasn't an enjoyable trip, especially for Charlie, who took so much pride in his own taxi service. Both taxis were in terrible condition and erratically driven by their reckless drivers. Charlie was amazed that taxis could be so poorly maintained, especially the one he was riding in.

"I've never been so frightened in my life", Charlie told Ada, once they were clear of earshot from the drivers, "Those cars should have been scrapped long ago!"

Lunch was taken at the tea rooms in the zoo, but it was something of a disappointment, only meat pies were on the menu and they didn't go down too well with any of the party.

Ada was quite tired by the time they had finished at the zoo but a relaxing ride back to Wynn's by ferry gave her the opportunity to recover in time for an enjoyable dinner and evening from her hosts. Another precarious taxi ride saw the tourists return to their flat at Fig Tree.

—

The morning of Tuesday September 2 was spent writing letters home and Charlie then turned his attention to servicing his faithful Hudson while the ladies attended to various odd jobs. Ada stayed

Another view of the new Sydney Harbour Bridge, this time taken from the Taronga Zoo.

The ladies enjoy a visit to Manly Beach while in Sydney.

at home waiting for the gas service man to come but he didn't arrive until 5:00 pm. Meanwhile Lil and Eileen headed off into town for some shopping, but not returning to Hunters Hill until quite late, missing the ferry by "half an inch" and then missing the bus as well was their excuse for being late for dinner. Consequently dinner was late and the rest of the evening was spent having a quiet night indoors listening to the gramophone.

—

More Sydney area touring was undertaken on Wednesday with a ferry ride to town first thing, followed by another ferry ride to Manly. Here they met Gladys Williams and lunched at the Astoria Hotel, after which Miss Glenny and Miss Wilmot went for an enjoyable swim. Miss Beal asked Charlie to sneak some photos of the ladies in their swimming costumes without them noticing, a feat he managed to complete with some amusement, but without detection.

A roaming photographer also took photos of the whole group, later showing them the result which Ada thought wasn't a bad effort. Unbeknown to them, this photo was to appear in the Sydney papers the next day, along with a story about the long taxi fare, much to their amusement. At the end of a lovely day it was back onto the ferries for the return to Hunters Hill for dinner and an early night.

—

The top of an escarpment in the Blue Mountains.

Cliff face in the Blue Mountains.

The reckless taxi trips apparently didn't cool the travellers' enthusiasm too much as they engaged another car to take them on a trip into the Blue Mountains the next morning. Good progress was made and they enjoyed morning tea at the "Log House" in Penrith, before continuing on to Katoomba where Miss Beal made a call on the local bank to change a cheque. Here she was surprised to find that the manager, Mr Wall, came from Camperdown, quite close to her own hometown and that he was a friend of Mr Johnson, the bank manager at Birregurra.

After cashing the cheque the party moved on to Blackheath for lunch at the Astoria, an establishment that Miss Beal and Miss Glenny had visited a couple of years earlier. They found it much improved from their previous visit.

Turning right out of Blackheath, their next stop was at Govett's Leap where the view was described as "breathtaking". The inspiring sounding name is sometimes attributed to an escaped convict turned bushranger who, pursued by troopers, found himself cornered on the edge of the high cliff. Rather than be taken by his tormenters, he jerked his horse's head around and plunged over the cliff. But the legend isn't true! In fact the Leap was named after the colonial assistant surveyor, William Govett, who discovered the site one hundred years before Charlie and the ladies made their visit.

On the return journey the "Three Sisters" rock formation at Katoomba was visited, along with the spectacular Wentworth Falls. As the evening closed in the party reached Parramatta where Ada and Eileen earnestly, but unsuccessfully, sought out another café where they had dined previously.

The Three Sisters at Echo Point in the Blue Mounains.

A view of the township of Katoomba in the Blue Mountains.

Misty view across the hills in the Blue Mountains.

An alternative was soon settled on, although not without some misgivings, when another patron seated nearby left his meal untouched, paid for it, and promptly left! Slightly bemused, Charlie and the ladies ate theirs with relish and suffered no apparent ill effects.

With dinner taken care of it was back to Fig Tree once more and another early night after a big day of touring in the Blue Mountains.

—

Next morning Lil and Ada went off to Hunters Hill first, then on to Vaucluse where they spent the afternoon with Gladys and Mrs Williams, staying on for dinner. While visiting, Gladys drove them to Circular Quay where they heard the improved large gramophone record by Gigli, featuring "The Serenade". Charlie, Eileen and Alice spent the afternoon doing their own sightseeing with Eileen's friends from Oriomo.

There were some more anxious moments for Charlie and Eileen that evening when Ada and Lil missed the ferry and arrived home very late. They were beginning to think something unpleasant might have happened to them.

Charlie spent the evening writing to Hazel once more. Having made it all the way back to Sydney, it wouldn't be long until he was home again to his wife and family, something he looked forward to eagerly.

View across Sydney Harbour.

—

The final day in Sydney was spent relaxing in the morning before enjoying lunch at the local Fig Tree Café. Then it was into two taxis again, together with Wynn and heading of to the National Park where there were hordes of Queensland Lilies growing to a great height. The mini convoy meandered along Lady Carrington's Drive and a stop for afternoon tea was made at Audley where Bell Magpies hopped about on the verandah, gaining morsels of food for their trouble.

After another enjoyable day it was back to Hunters Hill for dinner after which everyone packed their belongings, ready to leave Sydney the next morning. As much as they enjoyed the stay in Sydney, Charlie was eager to head south again, back to Hazel and the children.

■ **Chapter**

12

Heading for Home

A final

call to Hunters Hill was made to say goodbye to Wynn and then the metropolitan area of Sydney faded in Charlie's rear vision mirror by mid-morning as the adventurous party set off on the last leg of their amazing journey. No stops were made until the Bulli Pass was reached, 42 miles south of Sydney, where they all enjoyed the marvelous view from the top of the pass. Here they decided on a recommended steak for lunch and spent some time taking photographs before continuing on their way through Wollongong toward Huskisson on the south coast of NSW, for the proposed overnight stay. A suitable hotel, with rock lilies decorating the rooms, no less, was secured for the night and the travellers spent the evening walking along what Miss Beal described as "the most interesting beach" she had been on. The day was brought to a close with enjoyment of a substantial meal and all retired to bed early.

—

A 10:00 am start saw the Hudson rolling along what Charlie described as a "wonderful road" that took them to the entry gate of the Naval College at Jervis Bay where Ada was keen to stop and hopefully take a tour of the grounds. Cadets who would normally have trained here had recently been removed to Flinders and even Ada's best "Palm Oil" couldn't persuade the guard at the gate to let them in for a look around. All they could see was the main building in the distance.

Beautiful wildflower country was encountered on returning to the main road with Burrawong palms and ferns predominant. The late morning drive took the tourists past blackwood saw-mills and picturesque seaside inlets until lunch was taken at Batemans Bay, after a punt ride across the Clyde River inlet. Here there was a chance to gaze out to sea where the Schnapper and Crouching Lion Islands seemed to hover in the distance. Next the travelling party set their sights on Narooma for the overnight stop, but first they had to drive the Hudson onto another punt to cross the Wagon River inlet. The punt ride gave Charlie the chance to total up the day's travel – 127 miles.

Opposite the hotel there was an interesting shop where Charlie and the ladies amused themselves by playing gramophone records, succumbing in the end to the purchase of their favourite one.

—

Tuesday September 9 was the 82nd day of the journey and it started out from Narooma a little earlier than the previous couple of days, allowing them time for a stop at Quaama to send telegrams and purchase more supplies. Amongst the goods purchased were milk, some rock lilies and staghorns that

A view over the coastline from the top of Bulli Pass.

Kiama, south of Sydney.

Ada wanted to take home. The post mistress was very interested in the trip for she had learned of the three ladies in the taxi travelling to Darwin and back and offered to send the plants on later for Miss Beal. She was true to her word, sending them down in a parcel that weighed 18 pounds.

From Quaama they passed through range after range of beautiful, thick timbered country and enjoyed a magnificent view of Bega, about five miles before they actually reached the town. Despite the stops they were still able reach Eden for lunch. Oysters were on the menu for lunch and they were so delicious they all ordered more to take with them for afternoon tea at Gypsy Point on the Mallacoota inlet.

Just before the Victorian border Charlie was surprised by a bad turn at the Timbillica Bridge, but they negotiated it safely and stopped right on the NSW-Victorian border. There was a signboard on the border so Charlie drew the Hudson to a stop and celebratory photos were taken of the milestone occasion.

Gypsy Point was to be the overnight stay, but progress was good and so the decision was made to continue on to Mallacoota, where they spent the night. Total mileage for the day was 146.

—

Miss Beal hired a motor launch to take them up the Pergagoolah Lakes to Gipsy Point the next

Charlie hams it up a little on reaching the NSW/Victorian border.

morning where they landed to find that the hotel there was much better than the one they had chosen in Mallacoota. Not one to procrastinate over such decisions, Miss Beal immediately booked rooms here and headed back to Mallacoota where they were late for lunch. To make matters worse, Ada broke the news to the Mallacoota publican that they were cancelling their rooms and returning to Gipsy Point right away. He was not impressed.

Everything was packed up and loaded onto the Hudson for the short trip back to Gipsy Point, but a quick stop was made along the way so Lil and Eileen could get out and walk along to enjoy a better view of the marvelous wildflowers. On reaching Gipsy Point they could see Gabo Island and the wreck of the "Riverina" from the inlet. Afternoon tea was taken at the hotel and then Miss Beal once again engaged a motor launch to take them up the river on a fishing trip. Four young men provided the launch and assistance with the fishing, constantly baiting their hooks with vigour, but all to no avail, as the fish only nibbled, they weren't interested in taking the bait seriously. Nevertheless it was a very enjoyable evening, so much so that it was dark by the time they returned to the hotel. Eileen Glenny met up with some old friends in the evening to bring a wonderful day to a close.

—

The Hudson was still running perfectly as Charlie pointed it away from Gypsy Point at 9:00 am. Each day was taking them closer to home. A stop for petrol was made at Genoa and then it was on through heavily wooded flats to Cann River. From Cann River to Orbost the road passed through mile after mile of wonderful bush scenery, grand panoramas and gullies of tree ferns, massive tees and beautiful bush flowers. On reaching Orbost Miss Beal paid a visit to the bank to make use of her letter of credit. To her surprise the manager was an acquaintance from Birregurra who recognised her immediately.

Continuing on, the Snowy River was crossed and then a short divergence was made to visit the mission station at Lake Tyers. The gentleman in charge was reluctant to show them around at first, so they rewarded him with their left-over groceries and his demeanor changed.

Final destination for the day was Lakes Entrance, which they reached too late for a visit to the beach, but with enough time to allow a walk around town to be enjoyed before dinner at the hotel. Despite only travelling 122 miles for the day, everyone was tired so it was another early night.

—

After an early breakfast Eileen and Lil went by launch to the ocean beach where they collected shells and took in the beach scenery. They were back in time for a 9:40 am departure from Lakes Entrance, with a long day ahead, as the planned destination was to be Dandenong, almost home again! Along the way morning tea, lunch and afternoon tea was taken in the bush and they passed through Bairnsdale and Sale before making a short 5-1/2 mile divergence to marvel at the wonderful

The three ladies pause for a photo at Lakes Entrance, nearly home again.

new garden town of Yallourn, on the edge of the vast brown coal deposits being developed by the State Electricity Commission.

Once clear of Warragul the excitement started to build once more for all of the passengers as the undulating country afforded views of the South Gippsland Ranges with the last hints of snow caps melting in the Spring sunshine. Occasional glimpses of the Dandenong Ranges and Port Phillip Bay spurred their excitement even more, but they soon settled down on reaching the hotel in Dandenong as it was second rate at best, and it was the best of a poor lot.

Everyone was relaxing before dinner when surprise visitors walked up to Miss Beal's door. It was Mr and Mrs Murray, the same couple they had passed several times on their way to Newcastle Waters some weeks ago. They invited Charlie and the ladies to spend the evening at their house after dinner and even came in their own car to pick them up. It turned out that Mr Murray had seen Charlie driving the Hudson into the hotel's garage and recognised it immediately.

—

September 13, 1930 was to be the last day of this epic journey. Eager to get home, the Hudson roared out of Dandenong at 8:00 am, with an air of excitement permeating the interior. By 9:30 am they had turned into Burke Road off the Dandenong Road and soon they were outside Lil Wilmot's house in Camberwell to find that all Miss Beal's friends had been following their journey and were expecting them as they drove up. Jack, Bee, Harold and Nancy gave them such a warm welcome and Mrs Nettle also came by to welcome them home over morning tea, with much excited chatter about the trip.

The Hudson caused much interest in the streets of Melbourne and they were greeted by many admirers along the way. Some even applauded their efforts in driving all the way to Darwin and back. Charlie was a little embarrassed by all of the attention, but they all soon responded to the welcome home, dressed up in their travelling garb and in Charlie's own words, "put on a bit of a show". All the attention slowed down their progress somewhat so they were later getting to Geelong than anticipated. Imagine the surprise when they found the shop windows all decorated in yellow and black streamers, the same colours as the Hudson, that had so reliably carried them all the way to the top of Australia and back.

Poor Hazel and the children had been waiting over two hours for Charlie's return, so it was indeed a joyous occasion when the Hudson eventually came rolling down the street to greet them. There was quite a crowd on hand to welcome the travellers back home, many of whom Charlie knew, but also many well-wishers whom he didn't recognise. Still it was a great relief to be home. Three months was such a long time to be away from the family and it was sheer delight to see their smiling faces once again.

Soon it was time for Charlie's remaining passengers, Miss Beal and Miss Glenny, to say their very sad goodbyes. The trip had seen them all become such good friends and Miss Beal summed it up by stating that "the whole journey had been made under the most pleasant conditions possible to imagine". Charlie's heart swelled with pride as he hugged his loved ones once again and loaded them on board the faithful Hudson for the short trip to their own home. The world's longest taxi fare was over.

One final photo of the group on arrival outside Lil Wilmot's home in Camberwell, Melbourne on the morning of September 13, 1930.

Notes:

The Hudson weighed three tons 10 hundred weight, fully loaded with 40 gallons of extra petrol and 40 gallons of water, plus three containers of spare parts and 150 feet of coconut matting.

Charlie Heard arrived home on September 13, 1930 at 11:30 am having covered a total of 7,003 miles, using four quarts of oil and 505 gallons of petrol. Only one puncture was suffered and fuel reached five shillings and nine pence per gallon at the dearest point.

Finally, back at home in Geelong after 7000 miles in the Hudson, Charlie is reunited with his family, daughters Dawn, Norma and Vemba, wife Hazel, and son Mervyn.

■ Part
2

"What the hell, we will come too"

Foreword

The Heard family re-creates Charlie's trip

Our particular story started about 20 years ago when my Auntie Vemba (Charlie's daughter) came to visit, as she did once or twice a year. She came in and sat down at my table, in her hand was a very old looking photo album.

She began by saying, "Steve, I don't know if you would be interested, but this is my dad's photo album of his taxi trip back in 1930."

Straight away my ears pricked up.

Auntie Vemba continued, "Not many people knew about this trip when dad (Charlie) came home from Darwin, I was only about seven or eight, your dad (Mervyn) would have been about nine or ten. At that time there was a huge fanfare in anticipation of dad coming home, shop windows were painted cream and black, the same colours as his Hudson and there were streamers and balloons hanging everywhere.

"Mervyn and I were allowed to stay home from school for the day. Early in the morning, Mervyn and I, or I should say "Boy" and I, that's what we called your dad, because he was the only boy with six sisters, walked down to the corner to see dad coming home. We waited and waited. Every so often I would run back home and ask mum, when he would be coming. Her answer was, "Soon Vemba, soon".

"Anyway, back to the album, when dad finished his trip he had all of his photos processed, put them into the album, along with all of the telegrams he had sent to mum and luckily he wrote captions under each photo.

"I thought you might like to keep this album as a memento of your grandfather. The album had been misplaced in the bottom of my wardrobe for some 50 years and I only found it the other day. It is yours now and I hope it will be of some interest to you."

Flicking through the album, I could not believe my eyes. Straight away I knew this was of great importance to me, my family and my extended family across Australia.

Auntie Vemba was probably in her eighties by this time but she was so switched on that she knew names, dates, people, even little things that happened years ago.

With a hot cup of tea for Vemba and a beer for me, we started to chat about Charlie and his taxi trip. I quickly grabbed a pen and paper and started to jot down names, dates, places and quotations. Soon three or four hours had passed, my note pad was full and so was my brain. Auntie Vemba was amazing, if not for her this story would never have been told.

Weeks after Auntie Vemba came to visit I found myself looking through the album again and again, each time looking closer at the photos and discovering something new in each one. Soon this became an obsession with me wanting to know more about the taxi trip. I had all of this information on paper and in my head, so I decided to make a small booklet that included some of the photos, copies of telegrams and hand notes written down. This small booklet was then distributed throughout Australia via my extended family, just to show and tell Charlie's descendants what he had achieved in 1930.

Even Charlie's younger children, Dawn, twins Ray and Merle, and Wilma did not know of their father's achievement until my booklet came out. As mentioned before, the original album was misplaced for nearly 50 years and Charlie, being Charlie, was never one to dwell on the past. It was a paying job for him and he just did his job!

When my family and friends received this booklet some 20 years ago, they wanted more. I received phone calls and letters from all over Australia and even overseas. Their interest in the story was amazing and still they wanted to know more.

As the years passed my enthusiasm didn't wane at all and I decided I wanted to follow my grandfather's taxi trip all the way to Darwin and back by loading up my caravan and car and making the same road trip.

When I mentioned this to my brothers Ron and Bob, they said, "What the hell, we will come too." With three of us now keen to make the trip we thought to ask our sister, Anne and other brother Doug. With all five wanting to make the trip it was a different ball game. I suggested that

The nearest we could locate to Charlie's Hudson was this 1928 Essex tourer, very similar, but not quite the same as his Hudson.

we purchase a car the same as Charlie's original Hudson and drive it to Darwin. I asked all in favour to say "Yes" and there were five immediate, positive responses.

Now the hunt was on for a mid-twenties Hudson tourer but what we found out is that they don't grow on trees. The nearest we could locate was a 1928 Essex tourer, very similar, but not quite the same as Charlie's Hudson. The Essex was purchased from its Sydney based owner and brought back to Alexandra. The trip was beginning to take shape.

The Essex was stripped down and reworked, including the motor, gearbox, wheels, brakes etc. but the body was in perfect shape as restored by the previous owner.

With the Essex ready and five grandchildren ready to re-enact the remarkable trip, I suggested that we should film our trip and try to make a documentary of the World's Longest Taxi Fare.

After some hunting around we found a man in Brisbane by the name of Scotty Greasham who was an expert cameraman and an outdoor person who was up for an adventure. The date was set for 20 June 2008, exactly 78 years to the day that we would leave 61 Melbourne Road, Geelong at the exact time of 10:00 am. Why 10:00 am? Charlie left his wife Hazel, his children Mervyn, Vemba, Norma and Dawn at 10:00 am, 20 June 1930 from Geelong and headed to Lorne on the Great Ocean Road, Victoria to start his adventure of a lifetime and to pick up his paying customers.

With only three or four weeks to go before we were due to leave, there was a lot to get done. The Essex was prepared by Ron and Bob, without whose knowledge of motor vehicles, especially old vehicles, the trip would never have left Alexandra. More importantly we never would have made the 12,000 kilometre journey, for they had to work on the Essex nearly every day to tweak and fine-tune the old girl.

Brother Doug secured a four wheel drive that was serviced and prepared by Thompson's Transport, where Doug has worked for nearly 20 years. Doug asked Mr Bill Thompson if we could borrow the four wheel drive for a weekend and when Bill said, "Yes, of course Doug, you know you can borrow it any time you want."

With that Doug explained it might be a little longer than a weekend. "My brothers and I want to go to Darwin and back, and I will need about 10 weeks off work."

Still the answer was, "Of course, Doug, take as long as you want." Doug then explained to Mr Thompson about his grandfather's trip in 1930 and that we were going to re-enact the World's Longest Taxi Fare.

Not only did Bill let Doug have the four wheel drive, but he also helped in many ways before and after the trip. Without his four wheel drive the old Essex would still be stuck in sand somewhere north of Finke.

Next on our list was to try to find some sponsorship to help us travel the 12,000 kilometres. Numerous phone calls were made to companies I thought would be interested in helping. To my surprise these companies welcomed the opportunity, Yellow Express Taxi Trucks, TRJ Engineering, Dick Smith Electronics and numerous others came on board. The ball was rolling. Then after our story appeared in the *Herald Sun* newspaper, I received a phone call out of the blue.

"Simon Purssey from 13 CABS here, can I speak to Steve Heard?" Well from that moment on

A $500.00 caravan was purchased for our sister Anne to sleep in and cook for her four brothers and it was towed behind Steve's tow truck.

we made a lifelong friendship with Simon. We are forever indebted to him and 13 CABS for their assistance.

Back to our story. Essex – check, four wheel drive – check, Ron's Toyota – check. Now where is my sister going to sleep and cook for her four brothers? Okay, a caravan (a $500.00 special) will do the trick, I can tow it behind my tow truck. The tow truck, a 1977 Ford F350 banana back, was another back-up vehicle that would also travel the 12,000 kilometres. It was to be there in case of an emergency if the Essex, or any of the other vehicles had problems. To our surprise, and thorough, everyday maintenance by Ron and Bob, the Essex travelled the whole distance by herself.

Thursday June 19, 2008 at 10:00 am we were packed and ready to head for Geelong, anticipating another 10:00 am start from there the next day. With all of our friends, family and well-wishers there to wave us off, we left Rotary Park, Alexandra and to our amazement we had newspaper people and others we didn't even know wishing us a safe and speedy journey. When we left Alexandra, we encountered our first hiccup in the first kilometre – a flat tyre on one of the support trailers. No problems, Ron headed back to Alexandra to get it repaired and the rest of us kept on moving.

Mid-afternoon we arrived in Geelong at 61 Melbourne Road, which is now a motel site, where we were booked to stay for the night. To our surprise the motel was completely booked out. All of our relatives from all parts of Australia planned to give us a big farewell the next morning. What a night it was, family and friends reminiscing about old times and especially Charlie and his longest fare.

Friday June 20 was to be a momentous occasion with a 6:00 am start at the park opposite the motel. The *Morning Show* were preparing to do a live cross-over for us to talk about Charlie's and the ladies' original taxi trip and why we wanted to re-enact it. To our surprise we believe it went over very well, with well-wishers calling me on the phone over the next few hours with nothing but praise and messages of good fortune.

With 10:00am fast approaching, our goodbyes were said, hugs and hand-shakes received from relatives and friends and we were off to Darwin. On leaving Geelong, Doug did the first stint in the four wheel drive, Ron and Scotty travelled in the Toyota, Bob with a grin from ear to ear drove the Essex and I followed in the truck with caravan.

The CB radio was tuned to channel 18 as we chatted to each about our experiences so far and it was only the first morning. The previous night and this morning, catching up with our family members was still high in our thoughts.

As we cleared Geelong, with me bringing up the rear, I soon realised that we weren't holding up traffic as we suspected, we were leading a procession of well-wishers that followed us all the way to Lorne for our first stop. It truly was a sight to behold in my mirrors. There were Trevor and Lee in the old '55, Ron and Cheryl in the '56 pickup, Bob and Vera, Lester and Heather, Briggsie and a dozen more. It looked like a freight train heading to Lorne. Our first stop was 100 Smith Street, Lorne, where Mr Ulric Orr now lives, and has done since Ada Beal sold the house to Ulric's mother many years ago. With a warm greeting from Ulric and a firm handshake we were soon on the road again, but not before more filming and photo taking for the local paper. This is where our family and friends left us, it was to be an emotional farewell, for it would be another eight weeks before we would see our loved ones again.

At this point I was thinking of Charlie and how he had left Hazel and his four children, not knowing how long for, or even if at all, for Charlie's trip was far more challenging than ours. At least we had back-up vehicles and each other to rely on, Charlie had himself and three ladies, no back-up vehicles, no four wheel drive, no roads to speak of, and no RACV.

Soon we were in a rhythm, Doug leading the way and me bringing up the rear. We stopped at Birregurra at Charlie's old mechanical workshop and peered through the windows. We could all imagine Charlie inside, working on cars while our father, Mervyn played in the rafters and annoyed his father. On the road again our next stop was Colac where we had a quick bite to eat, for by now we were late to meet the Warrnambool Car Club and Camera Club at Flagstaff Hill Maritime Village and Musuem. Driving through heavy rain required our wipers in our vehicles on high speed. In the Essex they were manually operated so it had to be driven with one hand on the steering wheel and the other operating the wiper lever. Co-ordination was the key to keeping the Essex in a straight line and to maintain clear vision at the same time. This was to be the last time we encountered rain for the next eight weeks, only when we came down the coast near the Victorian border were they to be used again.

Camping out most nights was to be our priority for this was the way Charlie and the ladies had to travel most of the time.

Our first full day on the road and running repairs to the Essex were needed already. Weld up the shock absorber bracket and replace a headlight bulb and the old girl was as good as new again, thanks to Bill Poynton and the Warrnambool Car Club members.

By this time we were referring to the Essex as "The Old Girl", not to be mistaken for our sister Anne, even though we could not have done without either of them. The Essex was so much a part of this trip and with 13 CABS written on the door, people were starting to recognise the old girl as the old taxi going to Darwin, from nightly news broadcasts, shows and the daily papers. The other "old girl" was to look after her four brothers and photographer, Scotty for eight weeks on the road, with home cooked meals every night and breakfast every morning, all done on a two-burner gas stove in our "$500.00 special" caravan. How she achieved this we still don't know.

Camping out most nights was to be our priority for this was the way Charlie and the ladies had to travel, only every so often, in Charlie's case, staying in hotels. For us it would be caravan parks, mainly to shower and recharge our cameraman's batteries.

Speaking of our cameraman, (Scotty Greasham), he was from Brisbane and didn't we let him know it. Queenslanders know little about AFL footy, a fact that was proven time and time again. The niggling and joking was all in good fun and after eight weeks we had him converted to AFL, and that Collingwood was the best football club of all time. It didn't take Scotty long at all to become part of the family group, with his enthusiasm and sense of humour, he fitted in well. In fact he was soon to be introduced to people as our "other brother", Scotty.

Scotty had an eye for filming and still photos, he was also a very good bushman and could survive well in the outback. He would often prefer to sleep in his swag away from the camp, just to be by himself and at one with nature all around. It was only later in the trip that we realised he was a shocking snorer, hence his sleeping away from camp. I might add, at this point, there were a couple of others that would give Scotty a run for his money in the snoring department.

Scotty often demanded that we stop here and there so he could film certain parts of the trip, whether it was the old girl coming around the corner, over a hill, or through a river. Scotty would be there demanding, "No, let's do it again," just to get the right shot.

Soon this became known as "more bullshit photos" within our group, but if not for Scotty we would not have the hours and hours of film and photos in our own albums to remember the trip.

Steve Heard

Chapter

13

Family Re-enactment

Ron's Diary

THURSDAY 19TH JUNE – LEAVE ALEXANDRA – 263 kilometres:

We left Alexandra at 11:45 am and only got to the top of the cutting just half of a kilometre from town when a tyre blew on the white trailer requiring a return to town where we bought two new tyres. A large family group had met at Rotary Park to see us off. Finally we got moving again half-an-hour later and travelled out via the Goulburn Valley Highway to the Hume Highway in pouring rain and then to Geelong Road via the Western Ring Road. When we arrived in Geelong it was still raining. We met so many family members that we haven't seen for years, unloaded the Essex for some film and photos and had a meeting in our room regarding what would be required over the next couple of days i.e. to focus on the documentary and meet and greet afterwards.

We caught a taxi to the Gateway Pub for smorgasbord dinner (Vera and Bob shouted taxi and tea) and had a great meal. Caught a taxi back to the motel (taxi driver asked for my autograph). Had a couple of drinks with everyone in our room and headed for bed about 10:00-10:30 pm.

FRIDAY 20TH JUNE – 214 kilometres:

Up at 6:00 am, didn't sleep much all night. Lots of reasons, nevertheless up at dark, quick shower and wake-up the rest of the crew.

We walked over to Rippleside Park to organise what finished up being a huge send-off. People we haven't seen for years, can't name them all. There could have been upwards of 150 people. Steve's interview on Channel 7's *Sunrise* was wonderful from all reports we heard. We got away about 10:10 am and headed down the highway towards Lorne. Shelly and Murph, Kaz, Trev and Lee, Millsy and Cheryl followed us to Lorne in their old cars, to Ada's house where they said good-bye.

The road was good to Anglesea and along the Great Ocean Road to Lorne. We found Ada's house at 100 Smith Street Lorne and met the current owner whose parents bought the house off Ada Beal's Estate. We had a wonderful chat with Ulric. A short time later we headed off toward Deans Marsh and through to Birregurra, stopped at the garage (now engineering works) where Charlie Heard worked as a mechanic and his kids (Merv, Vemba and Norma) went to school in grades 1-3. We didn't stay long in Birregurra and then set off to Colac where we had lunch with us five, Michael, Scotty, Vera, Bob, Raelene, David, Kathy, Brilie and Billie. We said goodbye to Dave, Kathy and the kids and headed off to Warrnambool.

Drama started whilst I was driving the Essex. First the right rear lower shock absorber bracket broke off the rear axle and we had to stop, because the Essex was not tracking properly over the bumps (which is normal when a shocker is disconnected). We continued on to the Warrnambool Cheese and Butter Factory where we were greeted by Warrnambool Vintage Car Club and Camera Club members. We spent 45 minutes with these wonderful people and then drove on to Flagstaff Hill Maritime Village and Museum for the sound and light show. The Camera Club presented us with some little gifts and then we went to Cooper's Panel Shop to repair our broken shock absorber bracket (two hours work). While there we also repaired the left headlight. Eventually we made it back to the caravan park, had a light tea in the cabin and a couple of cold light beers and went to bed about 10:00 pm. Onward to Port Fairy and Mt Gambier tomorrow.

SATURDAY 21ST JUNE – 236 kilometres:
Up at approximately 6:30 am checked all levels on the Essex, had breakfast with Vera, Bob and Raelene who decided to come with us to Warrnambool then left the Surf Coast Caravan Park at 9:30 am headed for Port Fairy.

On arrival in Port Fairy we pulled up outside the former Post Office and had a look at this unbelievable old building, built in 1880. Charlie sent his first telegraph home from here. It's now a health food shop and after talking to the locals we discovered that just across the road was the original Jago's Garage where Charlie would have fuelled up. We also discovered that the present owner's grandfather was an Essex and Hudson dealer.

After looking around this old building, which is still a garage, we were escorted out of town to the highway by the garage owner's mate, who owned an old Jaguar. From Port Fairy we headed to Mt Gambier where we stopped for lunch at the Sinkhole Gardens. Doug and Anne had bought bread and sandwich fillings, so we made lunch and had a walk through the gardens as Charlie and the ladies had done in 1930. We had a cup of coffee and then decided to get a few more kilometres under the wheels.

Heading for Millicent we then turned off toward the small town of Tantanoola and discovered a park area opposite the Tiger Hotel. It is a disused railway station with fluro lights and power. We parked the car under shelter and set up our beds, also under the shelter. Walked over to the pub for a couple of beers, returned and lit the barbecue fire. Anne cooked vegies and Steve cooked the snags. We had a great tea and sat around the fire for an hour or so. Rang home, then had a nice early night in the swags, about 9:00-9:30 pm. We're heading for Meningie tomorrow, our third day, via the coast road.

SUNDAY 22ND JUNE – 247 kilometres:
Out of bed at 6:45 am, dressed, put Anne's kettle on and Pa's favourite "eggs in bread" on the fire for breakfast.

We left Tantanoola just before 9:00 am and headed off to Millicent, Beachport then Robe. On the way into Robe we saw a twin wing bi-plane doing joy flights, so we stopped and put Scotty in the plane from which he took some great aerial shots of the Essex travelling along the road towards Robe. We gave Ross, the pilot, a T-shirt and $70.00 instead of $110.00 and all was well.

The disused railway station opposite the hotel at Tantanoola provided our camp with fluro lights and power.

We parked the car under shelter and set up our beds, also under the shelter, walked over to the pub for a couple of beers, returned and lit the barbecue fire.

Driving into Robe we saw amazing old sandstone buildings that we caught on camera. We stopped at the Kingston Post Office and took footage of the Essex out the front. Filled up with fuel and headed off to Salt Creek (nothing there), so drove on to Policeman's Point and stayed at the pub overnight where we enjoyed great hot showers, toilets and soft beds. Hopefully we'll make Adelaide tomorrow.

MONDAY 23RD JUNE – 322 kilometres:
Left Policeman's Point Pub (between Kingston and Meningie) at 8:00 am and drove to Wellington, where we crossed the Murray River on a punt and then returned on the punt and drove on to Tailem Bend. We had heard about Old Tailem Town Historical Village from watching television the previous night. We stopped off there and spoke to Peter the owner. He was unbelievable, allowed us to photograph and film the Essex in the town itself, which of course no one else would be allowed to do. Running late at this stage we drove on to Adelaide and met people from The Advertiser newspaper, spent a few minutes with them and Anne's friends. Being later now than ever we went to Gawler and were very happy to be through Adelaide and heading north on the Barrier Highway.

We were stopped by a highway patrol policeman who picked me up for causing an obstruction on the highway. I twigged, by listening to the UHF radio, that Bob and Steve had set this up, so I milked it for all it was worth. (I fell out of the car making out I was drunk, slid down the side and sat on the running board, pretending I couldn't stand up. He asked if I had been drinking? I said,

All smiles with the Essex in front of our disused railway station shelter at Tantanoola.

13 CABS sponsored our trip and their logo became a ready identifier as we travelled along the same route used by Charlie and the ladies in 1930.

Driving into the Robe township we saw amazing old buildings that we caught on camera.

On the way into Robe we saw a twin wing bi-plane doing joy flights, so we stopped and put Scotty in the plane and took some great aerial shots of the Essex travelling along the road towards Robe.

"Yes, but got no idea how much, 'cause I'm too pissed". He made me blow in the bag, turned me around, told me to put my hands on the bonnet and frisked me – very closely – the funniest thing that's happened (still crying with laughter). I thanked the cop very much and said we would see him in Clare tomorrow. We stayed in Riverton Caravan Park overnight (cabin). Anne cooked vegies, Steve cooked rissoles and it was a great end to a wonderful, very funny day. We retarded the timing on the Essex to try to stop a noise in the motor and it worked great. Another big day tomorrow.

TUESDAY 24TH JUNE – 166 kilometres:
Stayed in a cabin at Riverton overnight, had a wonderful hot shower, followed by lots of fresh cooked vegies and rissoles.

This morning we were up at 7:00 am, made porridge for breakfast, gave the Essex a wash to get rid of the salt spray and headed off to Clare. At Clare we met the policeman's mate Peter that loved old cars. He has an absolute original, never been repainted, well surface-rusted Whippet and Overland that are both registered and have both done the Gulf to Gulf Rally. His workshop was a welcome site where we removed the back wheels, adjusted brakes, greased all shackle bushes and oiled the soft cork clutch. We drove out of Clare after Anne made sandwiches for lunch and headed north up the gulf towards Port Pirie.

We got to Port Pirie at about 4:00 pm after having to remove the brakes shoes from the right hand wheel because they again grabbed and slowed us down to under 60kph and overheated the brake drum.

We will sort the problem out at Port Augusta but Bob and I have to put our thinking caps on to sort out why this problem is occurring.

The owner of Old Tailem Town let us take photos and shoot film the historical village tourism attraction.

Meanwhile the Essex has now a comfortable speed of about 70-75kph and the brakes are fine.

Staying tonight in a cabin again, but as Charlie did, we will be in Bookaloo and start camping out from tomorrow night.

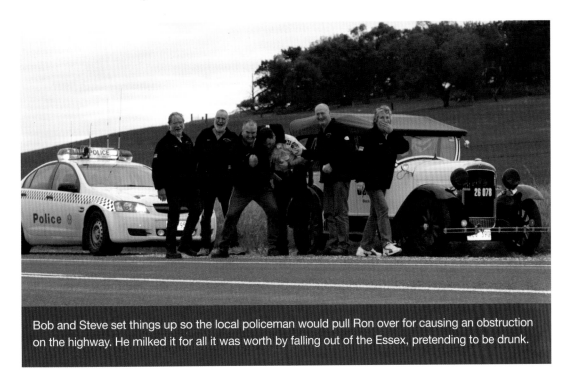

Bob and Steve set things up so the local policeman would pull Ron over for causing an obstruction on the highway. He milked it for all it was worth by falling out of the Essex, pretending to be drunk.

From left; Doug, Steve, Bob, Anne and Ron with the Essex north of Adelaide.

WEDNESDAY 25TH JUNE – 287 kilometres:

Had a great sleep overnight at the Port Pirie Caravan Park and Anne once again cooked an excellent meal.

We got away about 8:00-8:30 am and drove around Port Pirie before heading north to Port Augusta. We stopped at a railway bridge for photos and whilst taking the photos and then shifting the car up closer to the railway line the Ghan came along the track, which would have made for some amazing film.

We fuelled up all vehicles and again headed north toward Charlie's first campsite, a little place called Bookaloo where we stopped and made lunch with a cup of coffee and had a great chat around the fire. We stayed there for about 45 minutes then we moved on, managing to get the car bogged in the sand and it needed everyone to push me out and back onto the highway. We then drove through flat but wonderfully picturesque country all the way to a town called Pimba.

Pimba is six kilometres south of Woomera. We set up camp at a truck stop called "Spuds Roadhouse" at the Woomera intersection. There were covered areas where we set up the tarp and caravan, swags, fire, table and chairs. Again another hot cooked meal from Anne and we sat around a nice warm fire and sank a few cold stubbies. Got to bed about 9:00-9:30 pm.

The night will be spent in our swags in the open with the temperature expected to be zero degrees the next morning, hopefully we won't get too cold. Heading for Coober Pedy tomorrow.

The Essex in the Mallee scrub on the way to Central Australia.

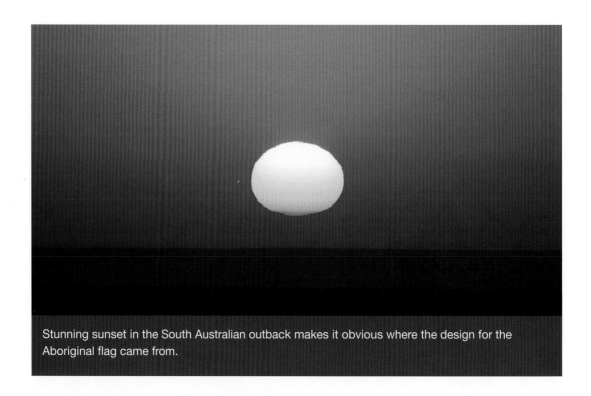
Stunning sunset in the South Australian outback makes it obvious where the design for the Aboriginal flag came from.

THURSDAY 26TH JUNE – 371 kilometres:

The night in Pimba was very noisy with trains, B-doubles and road trains rumbling past but we all got some sleep and were up about 6:30 am. Toast from the open fire with jam and billy tea or coffee was extremely enjoyable and warm.

We fuelled up all vehicles again and headed out onto the highway north. We stopped at Glendambo Roadhouse, about 114kms north of Pimba and had morning tea. Doug took over driving the Essex and said he managed, as he is 6'6" (198 cm) tall and 150 kilograms.

We came across an airstrip on the highway for emergency landings about 80 kilometres south of Coober Pedy. We also crossed a dry river bed just off the highway and the Essex handled it just fine. Then it was back onto the highway, driving through the Woomera Prohibited Area and into the opal fields of Coober Pedy, finally reaching a service station and onto a caravan park for the night.

A small repair to the alternator bracket on the Essex was required by the only welder in Coober Pedy after 5:00 pm. He turned out to be a lovely bloke, Ross, who couldn't do enough to help us.

It had been a very long day of 371 kilometres at 65-70kms/hr, plus three fuel stops and a very quick lunch stop.

FRIDAY 27TH JUNE – 0 kilometres:

As a lay-day in Coober Pedy, it was a very busy time. Firstly we went to Anne Johnson's bed and breakfast dug-out in the town, what an incredible way to live. She is heavily involved in the historical society of Coober Pedy and pointed us in the right direction to discover the original post office, Commonwealth Bank, general store, opal shops, original water tank (all of which Charlie and Ada visited), museum and the modern day post office and Commonwealth Bank.

We all drove up to the lookout, then to the tourist information centre and studied a wall map of where we are going over the next week.

We met two aboriginal guys who, in the end, convinced Bob to let them sit in the Essex. Then Bob took Cody for a drive. I'm sure it was the highlight of his life. He managed to spill half a stubby in the front of the Essex and it now stinks of beer. We also called into the underground pub and museum, that was amazing and my opinion of Coober Pedy has now changed for the better. We met Gary, the guy who owns the Coober Pedy newspaper and he took a photo of our car and said he'll put another story in the paper. Steve and I chatted to him about his reasons for living in Coober Pedy and he said that this town has everything except the beach.

Gary at 27 years old had lived in 27 houses and 17 towns, is now 62 years old and just loves his town of Coober Pedy.

Tomorrow we are heading outback and hopefully arriving in Oodnadatta mid-to-late afternoon.

SATURDAY 28TH JUNE– 198 kilometres:
Left Coober Pedy at 8.15 am and set out along the Oodnadatta track. Along the way we took a lot

We met two Aboriginal guys who, in the end, convinced Bob to let them sit in the Essex. Then Bob took Cody for a drive.

of film and photos of the landscape that could be on the moon. The amazing thing is that the change in the landscape was incredible over the 200 kilometres we had travelled. We were very happy with the way the Essex handled the corrugated gravel road.

We crossed several cattle grates that separate the cattle stations, some of which were thousands of acres in size. We also discovered two large water tanks, a huge windmill and dam. I guess the dam is what the cattle drink, although it was very salty water. We crossed a creek about 100 kilometres from Coober Pedy that was dry, but I can just imagine the huge flow of water in the wet season. I guess over the 8-10 cattle stations and 200 kilometres we saw no more than 40-50 cattle and God knows what they were eating, you could count the blades of grass on one hand.

We had lunch about 2:30 pm then kept on moving and finally arrived in Oodnadatta about 4:00 pm, had a beer at the pub and headed for the only caravan park behind the Pink Roadhouse, where we also filled our vehicles with fuel.

At the caravan park we opened up the trailer to see more dust inside than you could possibly imagine. About an hour later and after getting rid of kilograms of dust we set up camp, got the fire going and cooked our tea. We then washed tea down with many cold cans of beer, had a well-earned shower and climbed into our swags for hopefully a good sleep, because tomorrow I feel will be much the same!

SUNDAY 29TH JUNE – 28 kilometres:
Up early and a hot shower again to get rid of some more of the red dust. We packed up camp and then Steve needed to ring the pilot to organise some aerial photos. The crew took off toward Finke

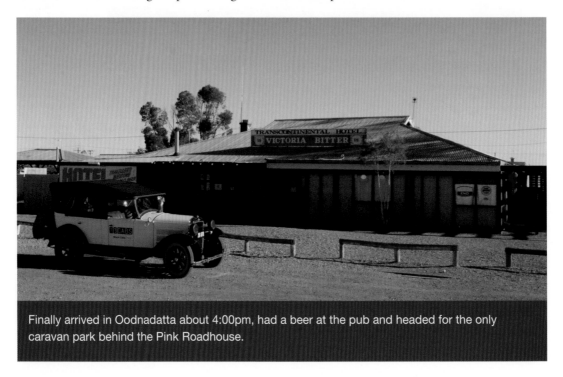

Finally arrived in Oodnadatta about 4:00pm, had a beer at the pub and headed for the only caravan park behind the Pink Roadhouse.

Sunset in the South Australian outback.

The road conditions varied dramatically, the scenery even more so, from red soft sand to gibbers (large rocks) and the odd creek bed.

Bores with windmills are the only source of water in many areas of outback South Australia .

Red dirt, gibbers and sporadic clumps of spinifex typify this part of outback South Australia.

The siblings enjoy a lighter moment in this abandoned old car in the middle of the outback.

We left Oodnadatta and headed out into nowhere on some of the worst tracks that we have ever driven on.

on the Old Ghan Track about midday and I stayed in Oodnadatta to repair our first flat tyre. The garage being closed on Sunday, proprietor Adam said, "Use what you want but I don't work on Sundays." Not ever having to change one of these tyres on a split rim before it took about two hours and a lot of swearing before it was all done. Prior to that the cameraman had to be taken to the airport to meet the plane and take some aerial photographs.

I left Oodnadatta after 3:00 pm and headed out into nowhere on some of the worst tracks that I have ever driven on and they have the cheek to call them roads! I finally met up with the crew at Eringa Ruins about 7:00 pm and over 1½ hours driving in the dark (something out here I don't want to do again in my lifetime). They were worried about my whereabouts and I was getting a little worried myself, believe me. But finally all was well and we had a late tea together and two beautifully chilled cold cans of beer before I set up my swag and climbed in.

The road conditions varied dramatically, the scenery even more so, from red soft sand to gibbers (large rocks) and the odd creek bed.

MONDAY 30TH JUNE – 80 kilometres:
Got up about 7:00 am had breakfast, packed up camp and then drove from camp right up to the ruins of Eringa, the original homestead of Sidney Kidman. Cannot ever imagine living here even though there was an amazing, large billabong on the Lindsay Greek where we took lots of photos.

We moved slowly along the Oodnadatta track and got to Abminga ruins where we crossed the old Ghan railway and siding for the first time since leaving Oodnadatta. Again we could have spent

We packed up our camp and drove from there right up to the ruins of Eringa, the original homestead of Sidney Kidman.

Camped in the desert, just like Charlie and the ladies, but with more vehicles and equipment.

Gnarly old gum tree at Lindsay Creek.

On the bank of the Lindsay Creek Billabong.

The Essex at Charlotte Waters ruins near the Northern Territory, South Australian border. Originally this was the site of a telegraph repeater station, post office and general store that was established in 1872.

Abminga Siding, now just ruins but with evidence of the old Ghan railway line scattered around.

all day here but we knew road travel would be slow and we had to keep moving. Our convoy passed through the border from South Australia into the Northern Territory and then on to Charlotte Waters – only ruins left here, so we kept moving through the deepest bulldust possibly imaginable. I'm thinking two feet (60cm) deep right across the road. We bogged the Hi-Lux support vehicle but the old Essex got through (due to large diameter wheels and skinny tyres I think). We drove through several patches of very deep bulldust but managed to get all vehicles through and finally into Finke (Apatula – the Aboriginal name). We drove around town looking for fuel and found a New Zealand lady and her son who run the fuel pumps, post office, pensions and dole cheques, plus the shop in Finke. This all closes at 4:00 pm and everything gets locked up, including a cage to lock up the fuel pumps. Because we needed fuel at 5:30 pm she opened up for us and we filled the old girl with petrol and some jerry cans and she told us where the campground was and off we went to the campsite.

Having set up camp, the New Zealand lady came out to see that we were okay and offered us showers in her house. We thanked her but couldn't impose and Anne cooked another wonderful meal (chow mein). We decided on an early night, as we are hoping to get to Alice Springs tomorrow.

I doubt we will make it that far because it's 240 kilometres or more on the roughest roads that we could possibly expect.

TUESDAY 1ST JULY – 80 kilometres:
Up at 7:00 am and cooked toast for brekky, had a couple of cups of coffee, packed up camp and went back into Finke from the camp site to get our bearings. The Alice Springs to Finke Desert Race

Time for Bob to enjoy a lighter moment on the abandoned railway line. Where's the roadrunner when you need him?

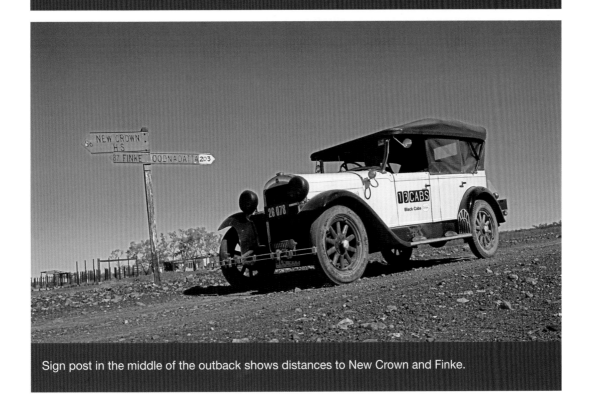

Sign post in the middle of the outback shows distances to New Crown and Finke.

An overnight stop at Finke gave us a chance to recover from some hard driving.

Bob and Anne re-create the scene shown on page 52 of Charlie and Miss Wilmot.

was held on the long weekend in June and they had cut up the Oodnadatta track terribly. So bad, in fact, that within 20 minutes from Finke we were bogged in sand. Between the Essex and the support vehicle we were bogged 12 times in 20 kilometres and stuck in sand many more times. We met several other vehicles going both ways, they offered help and knowledge on speed/sand and tyre

Reaching the Northern Territory border marked a significant point in the journey.

Animal remains are a reminder of the fickle nature of life in the outback.

The Alice Springs to Finke Desert Race had cut up the Oodnadatta Track terribly, so bad that we were bogged 12 times in 20 kilometres.

Dramatic evidence of how the Alice Springs to Finke Desert Race had left the Oodnadatta Track in terrible condition.

The Essex tackles a sandy section with some physical assistance from the boys.

Treacherous sections of the track really tested our patience because we had to dig ourselves out of sand bogs 12 times in 20 kilometres.

We were absolutely filthy dirty from crawling under vehicles and attaching tow ropes and digging metres of sand from around all four wheels on bogged vehicles.

The Essex plunges into the bulldust on the chopped up Oodnadatta track.

The Essex is through, but only temporarily.

The four wheel drive sign gives some indication of the conditions in the outback but the Essex still made it through.

Sunset over our desert camp at Bundooma.

pressures. To everyone who helped the Essex travel along the old Ghan railway our sincere thanks.

I was absolutely filthy dirty from crawling under vehicles and attaching tow ropes and digging metres of sand from around all four wheels on bogged vehicles. At the end of the day I just wanted to crawl into my swag and go to sleep.

Anne managed another amazing meal from inside the caravan after it had been whipping from side to side up the Ghan track and everything in the van was on the floor when we stopped at Bundoona railway siding. Calmly she put everything back in its place, cleaned out the sand and bulldust and produced ham steak and salad burgers. Only then did she start to cry. We didn't stop for lunch so two burgers each and another cuppa was extremely welcome.

I think we only travelled about 80-85 kilometres today but I never want another day as hard as this one and I'm too tired to even drink a can of beer. Hopefully tomorrow our spirits will be up and we will cover the 150 kilometres into Alice Springs for a shower and some time to clean everything, including our clothes.

WEDNESDAY 2ND JULY – 154 kilometres:
We left Bundoona railway siding around 8:30 am and got back onto the old Ghan railway line track where it was much of the same for a while, red sand and spikes. Over the next 36 kilometres we suffered no bogged vehicles, thank heavens.

Eventually we arrived at the Maryvale turn-off, the four wheel drive went to get diesel and we

Water tank at Bundooma.

View over Alice Springs from Anzac Hill shows the same layout as Charlie's photo from 1930 on page 70. Some of the original buildings are still there.

stopped at Rodinga for lunch and waited for Doug and Anne to return in the four wheel drive. After Rodinga the road improved enormously, some corrugations and sand but good going past Oak Valley and Deep Well turn-off and finally into Alice Springs.

Photo taken in the Todd River at exactly the same spot as Charlie did the same thing in 1930.

The Alice Springs Show and Camel Races were on so we had lots of trouble getting a powered site in a caravan park. The third caravan park offered us power from the house, which was much appreciated, so we could charge phone and camera batteries. We set up tents and rolled out swags, had another Annie tea and a couple of us walked up to the pub for a few well-earned cold beers. Nobody was really looking forward to cleaning red sand and bulldust out of everything in the morning, but we all knew it had to be done!

THURSDAY 3RD JULY – 0 kms:
Everyone was up at 7:30 am and did our washing for over an hour. Drove into town and got some brake springs and engine mount bolts. We also got a lower right hand side shocker mount bracket made – the same one that we repaired in Warrnambool. Put the old girl back together and gave her a grease and oil change, adjusted the brakes and hopefully she will be ready to go tomorrow morning. No kilometres in the Essex today.

FRIDAY 4TH JULY – 414 kilometres:
After a good sleep we were all up at 7:00 am, packed our gear, had a quick breakfast and headed up to Anzac Hill lookout with the Essex for some filming, then back on the Stuart Highway and heading north for Barrow Creek. There we stopped for a cold beer and a chat with the local

Essex at Devils Marbles.

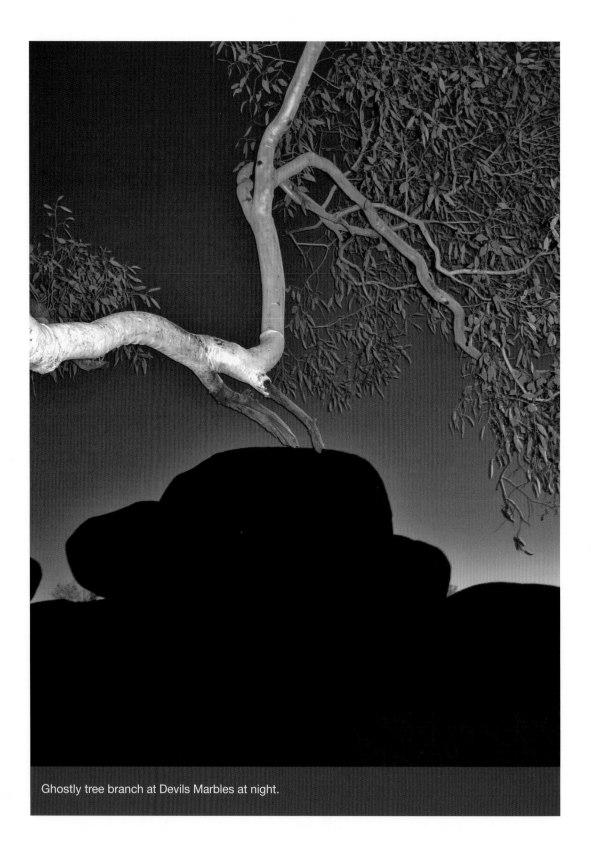

Ghostly tree branch at Devils Marbles at night.

aborigines. Took lots of photos outside and filmed inside the pub.

Drove another 10 kilometres north to the dry bed of Barrow Creek, discovered the old road and worked out almost exactly where Charlie's party would have camped. We took more film and then drove on to Wycliffe Wells, got some fuel and headed for the camp site at the rear of the Devils Marbles.

SATURDAY 5TH JULY – 267 kilometres:

Waking up at Devils Marbles was just the most incredible experience, the sunrise was spectacular and of course our cameraman was up at daybreak taking film and photos of the sunrise and the Devils Marbles. We met lots of people at this campsite who wanted to know more about our trip, and Charlie's original trip. Standing around the campfire, these people were just spellbound, staring into the fire and listening to what we had to say. At some time Scotty sneaked off into the large rocks that made up the Devils Marbles and took with him his didgeridoo that he had brought on the trip. He could play it very well. Suddenly, out of the silence and darkness Scotty began to play. It was the most amazing sound. Everyone just froze on hearing this noise, some even panicked and scuttled back to their caravans and locked their doors.

We met a guy named Dave that seemed to know aboriginal folklore and he told us that aboriginal men do not visit the Devils Marbles as it's a women only place (secret women's business)!

Nevertheless we made a cuppa and toast, got packed up and drove out of the campsite, continuing to take more film and photos.

We stopped at Bonney Well, just a few kilometres north, where Charlie stopped and commented that the water in 1930 was a little salty. It was replaced with a bore and windmill later on and the highway realigned but without this water Charlie commented that after driving for several days after leaving Singleton Station they were very pleased to discover Bonney Well and replenish their water supply.

After some filming we were again heading up north to Tennant Creek, where we stopped for fuel and some photos of the old car at the front of the Tennant Creek Hotel. Just north of Tennant Creek we made lunch and then called into the old telegraph station that takes you way back in time, to see the homestead, the smoke room and the cool store with a cellar to keep goods in the hotter months.

About 150 kilometres north we came to Renner Springs where we set up camp, had a shower and two cold beers at the bar before tea. Then Steve and Anne cooked chow mein again, which is a very simple, very healthy and extremely tasty meal. We sat around the fire for an hour or so and then about 9:00 pm retired to the swag. Although we only travelled 267 kilometres it seemed to be a very long way, compared to yesterday.

Hopefully we will get to Daly Waters or Larrimah tomorrow.

SUNDAY 6TH JULY – 415 kilometres:

We packed up, had breakfast and were on the road before 7:30 am, heading north to Dunmarra where we needed to stop for fuel at the roadhouse. We all drove straight past Newcastle Waters and turned into Daly Waters where we had a beer at the pub. Anne made sandwiches for lunch and we headed back out onto the highway and up to Larrimah. There was nothing there but a roadhouse with no fuel, so we only stopped briefly to put water in the old girl's radiator. A decision was made to keep going another 80-85 kilometres to Mataranka where we booked into a caravan park, set up camp and then drove down to the thermal springs and swam for a couple of hours in the warm water.

Back at camp it was hot dogs in bread for tea and another early night. A couple of hours in the morning and we should be in Katherine to look up friends of ours, John and Dianne. We should also meet up with the vintage car club there.

MONDAY 7TH JULY – 112 kilometres:
Left Mataranka about 8:30 am and drove out to look at Bitter Springs, then back into Mataranka and stopped at the police station, where we chatted to the female sergeant whilst waiting for the vintage car group to drive down from Katherine to meet us.

There was a great reunion with lots of laughs and then we headed up the highway to Katherine, arriving at Dianne and John's about lunchtime.

We took the Essex out to John's friend's place, who loves old cars because we suspected it had a blown head gasket. Noel, (John's friend) said just to flush the green additive out and then flush the engine with fresh water and air, then we filled it with water and Bars Leaks and set it at high idle for a few minutes.

Noel was confident that this would solve our problem, so we went back to John and Dianne's for lunch. After lunch Bob and I adjusted the steering (slightly more complicated than the other simple adjustment). Then I took the old girl for a run and came back more than happy with the steering.

We have a creek crossing early in the morning, taking the old road in places that Charlie would have travelled on prior to the new highway being built. It could be a challenge but at this stage we will just take it as it comes.

We were invited to stay at John and Dianne's place for the night and for tea.

TUESDAY 8TH JULY – 223 kilometres:
Our party left John and Dianne's about 7:30 am, fuelled up and drove to the low level river crossing of the Katherine River, where we filmed the Essex crossing the river (when it floods the water is 10 metres above this crossing).

We also crossed the Edith River on the old original road from Katherine to Darwin and the other major river in this area is the Ferguson River that we crossed on the highway. Our route took us north up through Pine Creek, Emerald Springs and Hayes Creek.

Here we turned back onto the old original road and travelled a further 65 kilometres into Adelaide River where we stayed at the showgrounds caravan park. We did a load of washing, had

Sunset at Devils Marbles.

On arrival in Darwin the Essex was driven until the front wheels touched the sea, then turned around so the rear wheels were touching the water, signifying the start of the return trip.

Sunset over Darwin Harbour.

In the long Mitchell grass, just like Charlie in his Hudson in 1930.

Road train dwarfs the Essex.

a look around town, bought the boys some stubbies and went back to camp. Anne cooked our tea and we had a nice cold beer before jumping into bed, hopefully for a good night's sleep.

Phone calls to home revealed all is well there. Whilst on the phone, my thoughts were with Charlie, for I could just dial the home phone number and talk to my wife whereas Charlie would have to write a letter and send it off. Days later she would have received it, no wonder Charlie was missing Hazel and the kids.

WEDNESDAY 9TH JULY –108 kilometres:

Left Adelaide River about 8:00 am and started on our last leg north to Darwin, a distance of about 108 kilometres. We achieved this without any bother at all. On arrival in Darwin about lunch time we drove directly to the wharf where we booked our seafood dinner. Then we found the boat ramp where we dipped the front wheels of the Essex in the bay, then turned the car around and dipped the back wheels. This was to signify that we have turned around and will soon be heading home.

Next we found a site at the Hidden Valley Caravan Park, set up camp and got ready to go out for dinner. We caught a taxi to the jetty restaurant and had a magnificent meal and then caught a taxi to the Darwin casino where I won a few bob. We then caught a taxi back to the caravan park, made a cup of coffee and jumped into the swag by 9:30 pm.

Small repairs are needed on a spring and the lights on the blue cargo trailer tomorrow morning and then hopefully we'll get some free time in the afternoon.

THURSDAY 10TH JULY – 22 kilometres:

Termite mounds south of Darwin.

Up early for a quick breakfast and then attached the large blue trailer to the Hi-Lux and headed off to get the slipper spring retainers rebuilt (they had worn the side out of both retainers). Called into Repco and purchased a set of points, distributor cap and condenser for the Essex and 12 volt white outside light for the caravan. Got back to camp and rewired the rear lights on the large blue storage trailer because the track had sand-blasted and ground most of the wiring away. Then we fitted the external light to the side of the caravan. All this happened whilst Doug and Anne went shopping, and Steve and the cameraman investigated and filmed inside the Victoria Hotel. The afternoon gave us time for some lunch and a drink.

We then took the Essex to Darwin wharf for filming and photos. From the wharf we drove to the Mindil Beach Market and had an incredible evening talking to people about the trip, the car and selling T-shirts. Left the market about 8:45 pm, headed back to camp where I enjoyed two cold beers and hopped into bed before 10:00 pm. No shower tonight, have one in the morning and hopefully get away early.

FRIDAY 11TH JULY – 310 kilometres:
We were on our way again before 8:00 am and heading south to Katherine after a very quick breakfast. Took some great footage of the termite mounds and the old car before stopping for morning tea at Adelaide River. Stopped at Pine Creek for lunch and some more filming and photo shooting. Then we drove the last 100 kilometres into Katherine to John and Dianne's block, where

A python makes itself at home on the radiator of the Essex at Dunmara Roadhouse.

we noticed the right-hand rear rim was split radially. We jacked up the car and changed the outer rim and tyre before tea and fitted stainless screws and glue into each wooden spoke to tighten the rim on the spokes. Put both wheels back together and left the car up on jacks till morning until the glue (two pack) set hard.

A barbecue tea at John and Dianne's together with one or two cold beers was enjoyed before we headed for a reasonably early night, sleeping in John and Dianne's bungalow.

SATURDAY 12TH JULY – 325 kilometres:
Woke early after a great sleep, had a quick breakfast and then we chased all over Katherine looking for an outer rim for the Essex – one has two large cracks in it. It was all to no avail so we fuelled up and headed south, stopping for filming along the way. Had morning tea at Mataranka, put some fuel in the Essex and drove through to Daly Waters for lunch and again searched for a rim without success.

After lunch we kept on along on the highway and stopped at Dunmarra about 4:00 pm for the night. Set up camp and then went to the bar for a drink. A lady called Helen was singing country music from 6:00-8:00 pm. Then we went back to our camp for dinner, a cup of coffee and then into the swag.

SUNDAY 13TH JULY – 250 kilometres:
Out of bed at 6:30 am, into the shower straight away and back to fry-ups on toast for breakfast. Then the roadhouse operator, Gary, bought out his python snake and we had a hold and let it go in the Essex, took film and photos. We thanked Gary for his hospitality because he didn't charge us for the site and he shouted the first round of stubbies last night.

Off down the highway we went to Renner Springs for lunch. We were not long back on the road when we arrived at Banka Banka Station where we decided to stop for the night. We pitched the camp and flushed out the Essex radiator that had Bars Leaks in it and replaced it with Chemi-weld. Hopefully this would fix our leaky head-gasket that was causing the Essex to run hot and dump about three litres of water the minute it got over 70 degrees. Hopefully we had fixed the problem and it wouldn't jeopardise the rest of the trip.

Chinese food for tea sounded good.

Went over to the slide night and took some film and photos of the car at the front of the old Banka Banka Homestead. After the slide show the owner invited us to tell the story of our trip and then we sold several T-shirts before heading back to camp for a quick coffee and into the swag.

MONDAY 14TH JULY – 457 kilometres:
After a great night's sleep at Banka Banka Homestead we were on the road by 7:30 am and heading for Three Ways (I went into Tennant Creek to get a puncture repaired, do some shopping and get fuel).

Caught up to the rest of the crew about 50 kilometres out of Three Ways and continued on to Barkly Station for lunch (our sandwiches and coffee). I jumped in the Essex to give Bob a rest and we drove to a roadside stop about 70 kilometres from the Queensland Border, set up camp and had a few

Leaving the Northern Territory for Queensland.

cold drinks. A young Swiss lad came over to invite us to his 21st birthday party at his camp.

Whilst celebrating his birthday Scotty pulled out his computer and managed to connect to the boy's mother in Switzerland, what an amazing thing! This lad is in the middle of outback Australia, looking at and talking to his mother halfway around the world. This was a great night sitting around a campfire chatting about everything and anything.

TUESDAY 15TH JULY – 288 kilometres:
Again all up early for a very quick breakfast, packed up camp and on the road to the Queensland border by 7:00 am. The sunrise was incredible and we stopped many times to take film and photos of the most amazing sunrise and sky that I've ever seen.

When we got to the Queensland border we took a lot more film and photos, because this was a significant point in Charlie's trip. Once into Queensland we kept on to Camooweal for fuel and a look around the old town. At this point Steve managed to get lost, we were calling him on the UHF radio but no answer. It was only when we happened to hear the local ABC radio station and Steve's voice telling the DJ and her listeners of the Longest Taxi Ride Fare and how we were re-enacting it that we worked out where he had gone. It was a big surprise to hear our story on the local radio. We headed off to Mt Isa and searched for a caravan park and found the last powered site in the town.

Pub in Cammoweal.

We all got the camp set up, showered, had some tea and went to listen to a lady reciting poetry. She allowed us to get up around the campfire and tell our story of Charlie Heard's longest continuous taxi fare. The poet, Carol, also started immediately writing a poem about the adventure as she was fascinated with our story.

WEDNESDAY 16TH JULY – 135 kilometres:
My previous experience in Mt Isa I didn't enjoy, but this time I was very impressed with the mining town.

We left Mt Isa after visiting the mine site, historical society and library. We drove through unbelievable countryside heading toward Cloncurry where we stopped again at the historical society. The lady at the historical society told us of a man in town who was 90 years old and may know something about Charlie's trip. Unfortunately he knew nothing about Charlie's trip, but he remembers events even prior to that and he was only 10-12 years old at the time. He had an old T-model Ford and a 1914 Willys Overland. His name was Billie Walsh and he was well switched on and a pleasure to talk to. His memory was faultless, he quoted model years, names and vehicles from 80-90 years ago as if it was yesterday.

THURSDAY 17TH JULY – 352 kilometres:
Six o'clock saw us up and well on the road by 7.15 am, fuelled up in Cloncurry, got some grease nipples for the Essex clutch and a globe for Doug's interior light. Steve spoke to Peter Weeks from our local radio station at home and then headed off to McKinlay (the home of Paul Hogan's *Crocodile Dundee*) known as Walkabout Creek Hotel.

We took lots of photos and film and had a look around town. (It's interesting that when the main road altered direction into town they shifted the hotel 500 metres around the corner onto the main road.) We had a cold beer here and then drove onto Kynuna where we stopped at the Blue Heeler pub. It was here we think Bob had a breakdown, or maybe it was just the heat of the day; he managed to climb onto the roof of the pub and pose naked for a photo. Not a pretty sight and I believe most photos were destroyed! We had another 170 kilometres to Winton so we kept the pressure on a little and got to Winton at 4:20 pm. It's interesting to note that Charlie and the ladies arrived in Winton at 4:30 pm on their trip.

We set up camp and then went into town to look for the Northern Hotel. All the names have changed and all three pubs have been altered, so we stopped at the North Gregory Hotel where a couple who met us at our last stop, shouted all of us two drinks each but Doug and Anne don't drink, so you can imagine the predicament. We took film and photos at the pub and then back to camp, showered and sat down to another wonderful meal cooked by sister Anne. Tiredness meant we would soon be in bed tonight. However I did walk into town with Anne and Doug and promptly lost $20.00 on the pokies.

FRIDAY 18TH JULY – 176 kilometres:
A late start today and we only drove into the information centre and historical society but it was well worth the hour we spent there as we got some valuable film footage. We also had a hot pie and cappuccino for morning tea and then headed off south to Longreach.

Along the way we stopped at a few interesting places and took film and photos as we went. Let me say the road between Winton and Longreach was a cemetery of dead kangaroos. There were hundreds of dead carcases spread all over the road. We met the car club five kilometres out of Longreach. These people were so hospitable and their old cars that escorted us into Longreach were beautiful.

Finally we arrived at Gunnadoo Caravan Park and booked in, set up camp and had a few cold drinks. We had been invited to the car club barbecue that night, just walking distance from the park.

We were made very welcome at the barbecue where we talked and talked, mainly about old cars. Then Bruce arrived with a 20-inch spare outer rim for the Essex and he just said to us, "make me an offer for it". He accepted a T-shirt and was very happy.

Our host John and Fay prepared a wonderful meal for which we thanked them and then back to camp and in the swag by about 9:30 pm.

SATURDAY 19TH JULY – 222 kilometres:
Took off to Bruce's place to adjust and grease the steering box about 8:30 am which made a huge difference to the steering. Then we went to Bridgestone Tyres and had our two tyres and tube (the one I repaired at Oodnadatta) fitted to the new rim, a job that took three tyre fitters 45 minutes. If you recall it took me three hours at Oodnadatta to change the first flat.

Finally they got the tyre and tube on the new rim and fitted it in the spare wheel rack of the old car. Next stop was the Qantas Founders Museum for filming and photos and then across to the

Charlie encountered a mob of 1300 cattle, we did the same thing on the re-creation trip, one of many coincidences.

Essex tackling a water crossing.

Australian Stockman's Hall of Fame for more photos and filming. We then drove to Barcaldine for lunch and then Blackall for tea. We stayed behind the pub in a caravan park. Here on grass we had a chance to fix the starter motor on the Essex – a bolt had come out of the Bendix assembly. We cut down another longer bolt and it fixed the problem, put it back together and then had curry and rice for tea before a couple of drinks at the pub and another early night.

SUNDAY 20TH JULY – 247 kilometres:
The caravan park was on a great site behind the Barloo Hotel in Blackall. Before leaving we added some more Chemi-weld to the Essex to try to stop the overheating problem.

Headed south from Blackall toward Tambo and met a guy from Adelaide who was into Essex cars, chatted with him and several townsfolk in Tambo about cars. Sold a few T-shirts and moved on to the park at Tambo for morning tea. Said goodbye to Doug from Adelaide and headed south toward Augathella for fuel and then drove through the back streets and discovered several stockmen who were moving 1300 head of cattle with 26 cattle dogs and 15 horses. These stockmen were the real deal Australian stockmen. They were droving the cattle from Alice Springs down through NSW to Swan Hill in Victoria.

We arrived just in time to talk to these guys about their life on the road before one operated on the near-side rear hoof of one of his horses with a pocket knife to remove a stick that had gone into the horse's ankle. After that they let the dogs off their leads, mounted the horses and moved the cattle out of the holding yards on to the grassy flats so they could all have food and a drink.

Stockman on his horse.

Great photos and film were shot of all of the above for about two hours. These guys had us mesmerised. We said goodbye to them and moved on down the highway to our campsite and almost had everything set up when it poured down rain for five minutes and drowned everything. After the rain stopped we dried everything as best we could and sat down to another lovely meal prepared by Anne and Scotty. Yet another early night.

MONDAY 21ST JULY – 256 kilometres:

What a night. Rain, lightning, thunder and road trains, it was hardly worth going to bed. Nevertheless we were up at 7:00 am, rolled up everything that was wringing wet and packed it in the trailer. Hopefully we would find some sunshine early in the afternoon to hang it all out to dry.

We managed to get all the vehicles out of Yo-Yo Creek roadside camp without getting any bogged and headed south again. Stopped at Morven for morning tea (pie and cappuccino) then off again to Mitchell where we called into the BP servo for fuel. Lovely people there gave us 5¢ a litre off $200.00 worth of fuel and four free stubby holders. They also told us of an old guy named Athol who had several old cars in his shed and took us to see them – what a collection. A Model Ford, '34 Ford, '53 Ford, '58 Star Model Ute, old Ford Fairlane and 17 tons of old car parts that he bought with him from Toowoomba to Mitchell, where he now lives. We spent an hour looking, talking and then back on the road to Amby where we had a counter lunch. Next stop Roma, quite a large town. We found a caravan park, dried out all the tarps, tents, mattresses and swags and things slowly got back to normal. Just needed a shower, a light tea and then we all looked forward to another early night, because last night we had very little sleep.

TUESDAY 22ND JULY – 277 kilometres:

Up again and on the road by 7:15 am, this time heading south to Dalby. We passed many small towns, a lot with silos for grain that became film and photo opportunities. At one spot we saw three people on a horse and buggy and that certainly provided filming and photo material.

The guy with the buggy actually built it himself and we spent some time chatting with him. We then drove on to Dalby and booked into the Miles Caravan Park on the creek and set up camp yet again. The owners of the park were very interested in our story and asked us if we would like to speak at their campfire and country music sing-song at 6:00 pm. It seemed everywhere we went people had heard of us and our story. There were people there that listened to our story in Mt Isa and were following us by accident but they came to the campfire and music night just hoping that we would tell them our story again. We had a great night around the fire listening to the music and telling people what our story was about. We finally got to bed about 10:00 pm, which would probably have been the latest that we had been to bed since our trip started.

WEDNESDAY 23RD JULY – 96 kilometres:

Expected it to rain overnight but it didn't eventuate. The road trains passing through Dalby kept us awake most of the night but we were up and away after some photos by the people in the park.

We back tracked through Dalby to the museum and historical society and spent an hour or more there, viewing a wonderful display of old vehicles and wares.

Back on the road and heading to Toowoomba and, of course, we had to come down out of the Great Divide on the largest hill the old car would ever want to come down (first gear from top to bottom). When we got to the bottom and wiped the sweat from our brows we stopped for cappuccino and pies at the small town where the car club are going to meet us tomorrow. We drove on further to a town called Helidon and camped at a roadside camp with toilets and fireplace and sheltered table and chairs for the night. Doug informed us there was a small country pub walking distance over the creek so I guessed that's where we would be going soon (before tea) and hopefully in bed reasonably early.

THURSDAY 24TH JULY – 133 kilometres:

Rained all night, everything by 7:00 am was wet, wet, wet. Spencer said he would be at our campsite at 8:00 am so we had to get up and deal with wet tents, tarps and get ready by 8:00 am, plus somehow have some breakfast before he arrived.

Took lots of film and photos and then followed the old road into Rosewood where Spencer lived, taking lots of film along the way. Well you should have seen his collection of old cars. Spencer, being a member of the Brisbane Hudson, Essex, Terraplane Car Club, had more bits and half-cars than I've ever seen in one place. We managed to reset our points on the Essex, study paperwork on the brakes of a 1929 Essex, pick up a head gasket, steering box, spare wheel, starter motor and many other bits for our Essex.

Had morning tea and lunch at Spencer and Wendy's and then we moved on to Brisbane and Logan in pouring rain. Finally got to Scotty and Amanda's place about 4:30 pm and set up camp. Whilst waiting for Scotty to return we sat in his local pub and when they arrived there was a surprise for Steve – Kaz came, Anne – Shelley came and me, Ron – Pam came and it was just a wonderful moment in our trip to see the three girls turn up with Scotty. We were all together now in Scotty's shed and looking forward to fish and chips for tea and a few cold beers. The girls have organised motel rooms for Steve and Kaz, Ron and Pam and Shelley and Anne. Bob and Doug are sleeping in Scotty's shed for the night.

FRIDAY 25TH JULY – No kilometres:

Pam and I woke at 5:30 am and watched telly for two hours this morning and of course enjoyed a cup of coffee. About 8:00 am Shelley drove us back to Scott and Amanda's and we immediately got started on the Essex steering box. After several hours we only marginally improved the steering after replacing the shaft in the steering box but it was as good as it was going to get. The next job for Scott and I was to go and pick up my Hi-Lux that should have had the valve replaced in the gas tank. After some delay and $200.00 I picked up the Hi-Lux and followed Scott back to his house.

We just sat and chatted for hours and finally we had a lovely homemade pea and ham soup and fresh rolls for tea that Amanda had been cooking for some time. After tea we sat around the fire for an hour or so and thoroughly enjoyed a very relaxing day. About 8:30pm Shelley took us back to the motel for some TV, shower and an early night.

SATURDAY 26TH JULY – approximately 80 kilometres

Up and out of the motel by 8:00 am to find Shelley has locked the keys in the hire car but RACQ had it all sorted before 9:00 am. Back to Scott and Amanda's for a quick tinker with the Essex and then off to McDonald's at Springwood to meet Duncan and Channel 7, then onto Kangaroo Point for filming, photos and Channel 7's interview. We finally arrived at the Breakfast Creek Hotel an hour late for lunch.

What a fantastic reception we got from friends and family when we arrived. The hotel supplied our meal free of charge, organised by Duncan, who was just wonderful to us on the day. Duncan is a guy who got in touch with Steve and I some weeks before we left Melbourne and was fascinated with the story in the *Herald Sun* newspaper in Victoria, and wanted to come on board with us in any way possible.

On top of organising the day he also raised some $500.00 sponsorship towards our trip from local businesses in his hometown of Caloundra, Queensland.

After a great day we still had a spit roast tea to go to at Scott's mate Steve's place. He produced a huge meal for us. We were also able to watch the 6:00 pm news on Channel 7 and see our

Arrival in Brisbane.

Time to leave Brisbane.

interview in Brisbane. It had been an unbelievable but long day, and we were very happy to be heading for the swag about 10:00 pm.

SUNDAY 27TH JULY – 195 kilometres:

Everything was packed up and we left Scott and Amanda's at Logan, near Brisbane, and after sorting out the tollways and freeways we headed south to a spot called Hastings Point that overlooked the ocean from Australia's easternmost point. We all had a chat about what Charlie would have thought when he and the ladies arrived at this point. They, I'm sure would have been amazed at the view from north of Surfers Paradise to Australia's easternmost point to the south.

From here we headed down the Pacific Highway to Ballina South, recommended to us by a fisherman from Hastings Point – crossing into NSW along the way. We turned off the highway at the Big Prawn in Ballina and headed to the ferry on the old original concrete highway that Charlie would have travelled on. Here we said goodbye to Amanda, Scottie's wife as she had to head back to Logan for work. We crossed the inlet on the ferry as Charlie would have and headed to the caravan park for the night. Bob and I were determined to figure out the vibration in the Essex and Doug and Steve went to catch a fish for tea, which Charlie also did on his trip.

We were told that if we ordered our tea before 4:00 pm we wouldn't have to cook our meal tonight because the kiosk/office has the best fish and chips on the north coast of NSW. I doubted that Doug and Steve would catch anything and they proved me correct!

MONDAY 28TH JULY – 258 kilometres:
Bob decided to wake everyone up at 6:15 am for some stupid reason. We had to wait for the park to open at 8:00 am anyway so we sat around drinking coffee and eating toast until 7:55 am. Eventually we made it onto the road after keys were handed in to the park owner and we headed south.

We stopped at a small post office in a town called Empire Vale to take film and photos and the school teacher from the primary school asked if we would mind telling the taxi story to the kids, all 55 of them. Well, they loved the story, we showed them the old car, gave them all little token gifts that were given to us by Simon from Black Cabs and after an hour of talking and questions, the principal and the teachers thanked us and we were on our way.

We headed down to a river port town on the Clarence River called Maclean and had a look around the port and the town and were soon on our way again to Grafton for lunch – more fish and chips. Leaving Grafton we drove down toward Coffs Harbour to a small roadside stop about 25 kilometres south of Grafton, set up camp, worked on the support vehicle for an hour, had some tea and yet another early night.

We fitted new points and condenser to the Essex just north of Grafton, tuned the timing as it started missing going up hill under load – this fixed the problem and she ran like a dream for the

School children at Empire Vale.

rest of the day. We tried to get parts for the support vehicle's brakes in Grafton but couldn't, however we managed to get parts to fix it temporarily at a truck yard.

TUESDAY 29TH JULY – 271 kilometres:
The worst night sleep we've had since we left home, the overnight stop where we stayed had a freeway on one side (the Pacific Highway) and the main railway line from Sydney to Brisbane on the other side of us. Five trains went through our tent, I'm sure of it. It sure sounded like they did and hundreds of trucks travelled over the bridge on the highway all night.

We got out of bed at 6:00 am and no one had enjoyed much sleep, so a quick breakfast was prepared before we packed up camp and were on the road by 7:30 am heading for Port Macquarie. We had to meet John and Pam Kerr and the Port Macquarie Vintage Car Club at Settlement Point, just north of Port Macquarie, which we did and went into a cafe for coffee and a chat. Channel 9 met us here and interviewed us and filmed the whole group.

We then drove in convoy from Settlement Point to Port Macquarie and through to the marina car park for film and photos, it was raining so much that we didn't bother and went back to the caravan park where we booked a cabin for two nights.

John and Pam then went and bought pies and sausage rolls for lunch, so we sat in the cabin and ate them. After lunch it was definitely clothes washing, drying and shower time for all of us. Tonight we are hoping to go out with John and Pam to the bowls club for a smorgasbord tea. I had been there before and it's a great choice with plentiful food. I was looking forward to that and a catch up with John and Pam.

We broke an oil line on the Essex so we temporarily repaired it and got back our 4psi oil pressure that stopped the rattle in the motor. We were convinced this time that we had run a bearing, or worse, but with 4psi reinstated all was well and we were off again.

WEDNESDAY 30TH JULY – No kilometres:
It was a great meal at the bowling club and home into a cabin for a wonderful sleep. Up at 7:00am and went for a walk down to the jetty and boat ramp in lovely sunshine. Had to be at the first high school at 10:00 am to tell the students about the taxi story, which they were extremely interested in and asked lots of questions. We were at the two high schools just after midday for a similar talk about our trip. Lots of photos and film were taken at both schools. Later we took some film of the shores of Port Macquarie with the waves and surfies.

We had a couple of well earned drinks in an Irish pub and then we put the Essex on the punt and crossed the river both ways. We also organised all-you-can-eat seafood night at the Port Macquarie Bowling Club, had a small dabble on the pokies and then home for coffee and an early night by 8:30 pm.

John and Pam moved to Port Macquarie some years ago from Alexandra, our hometown. Without John and Pam's help in organising the schools and the car club to greet us, it probably would not have happened and we would have bypassed Port Macquarie.

THURSDAY 31st JULY – 210 kilometres:

Knowing we had to leave early today we were on the road by 7:30 am and out onto the Pacific Highway heading for Tuncurry/Forster. Weren't we glad we turned off and took the coast road and went into Forster where we took some amazing photos and footage of the Tuncurry/Forster bridge and marina. What a beautiful place. On my previous visit to Tuncurry/Forster I commented to Pam what a beautiful place it was, in fact Pam said she could live in either one of these towns.

Coming out of Forster we came across another beautiful place called Elizabeth Bay in the Booti Booti State Forest. Even further on at another roadside stop we had lunch and chatted to an 80-year-old bloke who lived here for 30 years and told us that his neighbour caught fish only 10 metres from this wayside stop. It was another place that I would like to visit again. After leaving the beach road, the Essex ran out of petrol in the worst possible place that you could imagine, heading up hill, double lines, on a very windy road. However, with walkie talkies and stopping traffic and patient drivers we put 20 litres in and got going again. We got back onto the Pacific Highway and put a few kilometres under the wheels. At a roadside stop called 12 Mile Creek we set up camp, lit a fire, cooked some tea and hopped into bed. We expected a noisy night (trucks) and not a lot of sleep.

FRIDAY 1ST AUGUST – 111 kilometres:

What a shocking noisy night, there were probably 200-300 trucks, stopping slowing down and accelerating all night, so no-one got any sleep. Nevertheless we got under way after breakfast by about 7:30 am and headed down the Pacific Highway to Newcastle. It was a little tricky driving in and around Newcastle at peak hour in the morning but slowly we got through to the south side of Newcastle. We stayed on the coast road down to The Entrance then a little further south to a small town called Long Jetty, where the owner of a cabin park approached us and offered to help us with directions. He also (knowing the story) from the previous night's news program, offered us a cabin for the night as it was freezing cold and windy outside and not really tent weather.

Our cameraman Scott is cooking tonight in the cabin (stew and spud mash) so until dinner time we went up to the pub and had a few cold beers in a nice warm environment. Scotty's meal was just perfect, all eaten before a shower and then bed. We have a very early start tomorrow to get through Sydney and south to Gerroa to meet Peter and Anne to stay the night there. Scott and I are going over Sydney Harbour Bridge for filming purposes, only the others will go via the freeway as Charlie actually crossed the harbour on a punt. The bridge was not yet completed in 1930.

What a horrible night's sleep! A drunken fool and his wife fought and swore till 11:00 pm, throwing all sorts of things at our cabin and finally the park owner turfed them out at 11:30 pm. They left with four kids in a maxi taxi (how sad for the little kids). I don't know what would have happened if Doug had caught him. He chased after him down the main street in his jocks, all 6'6" (198cm) and 150 kilos, one hand on his chest complaining of a heart attack, the other fist in the air yelling, "Come back here, you little bastard, I'll kill you". At the time it was not funny, but by the next morning we were having a good laugh with our vision of Doug running down the road.

The amazing freeway just outside Wollongong.

South coast of NSW.

SATURDAY 2ND AUGUST – 262 kilometres:

After our second, almost sleepless night we got up at 6:00 am, made a quick coffee, toast and packed up to be on the road before 7:00 am. After leaving Long Jetty early we were back on the Pacific Highway and heading south, knowing that in about an hour or so we would split up and the Essex, Doug and Steve would travel the M7 to the south of Sydney and Scott and I would drive into Sydney, as Charlie did, to photograph and film the bridge from Taronga Zoo, the harbour bridge itself, the opera house and botanical gardens. After that we tried to get out of Sydney and got hopelessly lost south of the bridge.

We finally sorted it out after 1½ hours and got to meet up with the others at Coal Cliff (Swanson Park) and then travelled that sea road out over the ocean and at the foot of huge cliffs. We took lots of photos and film all the way along this coastline. We bypassed Wollongong and finally headed down the Pacific Highway and turned off to a lovely coastal road through several small towns and stopped overlooking a little town called Gerroa. Again lots of filming and photo taking took place along the way. We booked into a small park right on the beach at Seven Mile Beach and set up camp right next to the sand dunes. Bob did what Bob does best, he did a deal with the girl at the desk and we paid only a powered site for two people at $35.00. We went for a walk on the beach but it was freezing so that didn't last long, back to camp where Anne cooked vegies and we drank sherry. Steve cooked rissoles outside on the gas barbecue so we were all looking forward to tea and hopefully a good night's sleep.

I did not enjoy driving through Sydney at all, but loved getting the footage from the zoo, the bridge and the opera house. But the coastal road of cliffs, waves and scenery was well worth the diversion through Sydney.

SUNDAY 3RD AUGUST – 230 kilometres:
All had a lovely sleep in this morning and then up for breakfast, shower and meet Steve's brother in-law Peter and his daughter Stacey. Had a coffee and a chat then went for a walk on the Seven Mile Beach (the beach from which Charles Kingsford Smith took off to fly to New Zealand.

We were on the road by 9:30 am and heading south again to Ulladulla and Batemans Bay for lunch. Leaving Batemans Bay we travelled on the old Princes Highway along the coast to Narooma and booked into East Waterfront Caravan Park. We set up camp and then rang Uncle Doug and Aunty Dawn, organised to go around to their place and have a cuppa and a chat about Charlie and the trip. Aunty Dawn is one of Charlie's daughters and never knew anything about Charlie's taxi fare, as was the case for most of Charlie's kids. We went to the bowling club for Chinese food and a few cool drinks in Narooma where the night was very cool (a good reason for an early night).

At Batemans Bay, Doug Berryman gave me Charlie's World War 1 replica medals. Charlie had lied about his age to be eligible to sign up. He was only 16 and was sent to France. For a 16 year old country boy from Numurka Victoria, this would have been a harrowing experience at such a young

Dromedary Hotel at Tilba.

Back in Victoria.

age. Nevertheless he pulled through it and returned to Victoria to work on the Great Ocean Road.

MONDAY 4th AUGUST – 96 kilometres:
Rain poured down overnight and our tents and chairs got very wet. Everybody was up about 7:15 am and packed up almost all the camp but left the tents and a few chairs in the sun to dry.

Doug, Dawn and Heather came around for morning tea and a long chat about Charlie's trip. We heard of Dawn's knowledge of the trip, which was very limited, mostly as described in Steve's little booklet of some years ago.

We finally got on the road about 10:00 am and without exception we stopped every few kilometres for some of the best coastal footage that you could imagine. This was the case all the way down the coast past Bermagui, Tathra and to our campsite just south of Tathra on a salt lake. One town on the way we called into, which the old Princes Highway passed through, was Tilba Tilba. This is an historical town more than 115 years old and Charlie would have passed through here 78 years ago. We took a lot of film and photos of this amazing little town and, of course, had a cold beer in the old town pub.

We set up our camp. Steve and Doug went fishing, Bob and Doug put up the tents and I was talking to a local family about this beautiful place. He suggested that we drive further down along the lakeside to the sand bar that blocked the entrance and cross the sand bar to the Pacific Ocean. I did just that and found an area of Australia that very few people will ever get to see. I suggested to the rest of the crew that we go back to this area early in the morning for film and photos. Another 20 minutes around the fire chatting about this incredible day and I was ready for bed.

We were expecting rain overnight but we set up on sand so it didn't trouble us too much.

TUESDAY 5th AUGUST – 139 kilometres:

Let me tell you the rain truly was a problem. We got saturated wet, everything wet but we still had to pack it all up in the pouring rain, even though we waited for an hour for the rain to stop.

We finally got away from Wallangoot Lake about 8:30 am, had a photo taken for the local paper (in the rain) and then headed south on the Princes Highway to Eden where we stopped for fuel and coffee and then headed for the Victorian border.

It was exciting to get back into Victoria so at the border we took photos and film just as Charlie and the ladies did. With our excitement of reaching this milestone, we could only imagine what Charlie was thinking at this point. Soon to be in the arms of Hazel and the kids, not long now Charlie! After crossing the border and it still raining, we made our way into Mallacoota and drove down to the wharf. Two guys were repairing the jetty (replacing boards) and gave us the old boards that they cut up for us into foot long blocks for firewood. We approached the caravan park manager to see if we could hire the camp kitchen for the night and try to dry all our gear. After several phone calls to the shire and telling them the taxi story, they finally said we could hire the camp kitchen, and we soon had fires going to dry out all of our gear.

A hot shower, dry gear and warm place to sleep made for a good feeling. For tea we have mashed spuds, vegies and barbecue snags plus apple pie and custard for sweets and hopefully a nice warm night.

At the border between NSW and Victoria.

The Essex and a boat at Gipsy Point.

WEDNESDAY 6th AUGUST – 246 kilometres:

What a great camp place Mallacoota camp kitchen provided, we had a fantastic sleep and rose early to eggs on toast for brekky with coffee. It was a nice change to pack up quickly and have everything dry, so we were on the road by 8:00 am.

We drove a short distance from Mallacoota to Gipsy Point where Charlie and the ladies visited by boat, but they also drove there the next day and stayed in an old pub. Unfortunately the old pub has been pulled down and very flash units now take its place. There's no campground either at Gipsy Point and therefore it's now a lovely little place but only for the wealthy.

We left here and went back to the Princes Highway at Genoa and travelled through Orbost, Cann River, Nowa Nowa and reached Lakes Entrance for a late lunch. Lakes Entrance must have been an oasis for Charlie and today it's still an incredible place, I've heard it said that hundreds of tourists stay in Lakes Entrance every night.

After lunch we headed up hill out of Lakes Entrance to the lookout area and took more film and photos and then travelled on to Bairnsdale, through Tambo River and Nicholson River, to settle for the night in Bairnsdale (in a cabin not in tents). Tea tonight will be simple franks in bread I think and then early to bed.

We have only one more night to go and then into Geelong hopefully by Friday late afternoon. It is coming up seven weeks since we left home and we're all getting quite weary.

THURSDAY 7TH AUGUST – 267 kilometres:

Another ordinary sleep in a bed that was too short, in an ordinary cabin, so getting up early didn't trouble me at all. After a quick breakfast we left Bairnsdale about 8:30 am.

Nearly home again.

We travelled toward Melbourne on the Princes Highway, stopping at Rosedale for morning tea and fuel and then onto Yarragon Village where we met a B-Double truck loaded with logs that was heading for Geelong. He was stopped at a service station and we took film of the Essex parked next to this massive truck. Then the truck driver said he would travel down the highway a few kilometres, stop and wait for us (the photographer) and the Essex. We set up the Essex passing the log truck, which made great film and photos.

This was just another incident on our 12,000-kilometre journey (and there were many of them) that got me thinking about Charlie again. Charlie was always on our mind during the whole trip. How he did this or how he did that. But you will recall that Charlie and the ladies had to pull over to let the bullock team hauling logs pass just south of the Victorian border, not more than 50 kilometres from where we are right now.

After that we drove through to Drouin and stopped at a little campsite on the Tarago River for lunch. This brought back memories of early days camping with our dad in this exact spot and we pondered whether knowing that Charlie passed within 100 metres of this spot might have actually stopped here too. I guess we'll never know for sure.

The next leg of our journey is into Dandenong for the night to stay in a caravan park in tents for the second last night. Tomorrow we plan on calling into Huntingdale to see Thomo (Doug's boss) and then onto Oakleigh to see Simon from 13 CABS (our sponsor). Anne is cooking tea and we are sitting around the fire and I'm sure after tea we won't be long out of bed. We're really looking forward to tomorrow afternoon.

FRIDAY 8TH AUGUST – 112 kilometres:

In Dandenong overnight it rained on our tents for the last time. Nevertheless we packed up and were on the road by 8:00 am. First stop was Billy Thompson's truck yard in Huntingdale (one of our great sponsors) where we stopped and had a cuppa with him, Thea and his staff and a chat about the trip.

We then had to go to 13 CABS in Oakleigh and met Simon and his staff where he put on a real spread for us. We met his CEO who became one of our major sponsors, being convinced by Simon that the whole project would be beneficial to 13 CABS and obviously us. Simon showed us how the call centre for 13 CABS worked and it was truly fascinating and very busy. After a couple of hours with Simon we said our goodbyes because we still had to drive another 80 kilometres to Geelong, where Charlie started his trip. We arrived at the same place we left 49 days ago (seven weeks) at about 1:30 pm and took more film and photos of our arrival at our motel.

We parked all the vehicles for the night, sat in the sunshine and had a couple of cold beers to celebrate our return to Geelong. We reminisced about the trip that took us seven weeks and the hundreds of friends we met along the way, plus the amazing places that are out there to see in this fascinating country of ours. We now have a few hours to relax and then we are going out for tea to the Gateway Inn in Geelong. I don't think tonight will be very early to bed.

Total distance travelled – 10,557 kilometres, and the old Essex did every single one under its own power, the tow truck was not needed, other than to tow the old caravan.

Stark contrast of the damp track compared to the dry dusty outback.

The Essex made it all the way under its own power.

SATURDAY 9TH AUGUST:

We did have a fairly late night but were well aware that we had to be up early and heading for home (Alexandra) by 8:30-9:00 am. We took film and photos of leaving Geelong and loading the Essex onto the tow truck, as it had completed its journey that Charlie did from Geelong-to-Geelong.

We said goodbye to our friends in Geelong and had mixed feelings driving back to Alexandra. When we arrived in Alexandra at Rotary Park we were greeted by family, friends and grandchildren who were very happy to see us back. The reunion was a great time and everyone seemed excited and happy.

After an hour or so we had to go back to Steve's shed and start to unload our individual personal stuff from the vehicles and trailers and have the afternoon off. We were going out for tea with the family to our local hotel to celebrate our seven-week adventure.

It was a very hard time, in a way, having to keep to a schedule and packing up tents, swags, and breakfast every morning before spending several hours in unknown terrain travelling at 60-70kph, all the time being conscious of speeding cars, trucks, road trains that travel, in places up to 130kph, about double our speed.

May I say that 99 per cent of drivers of both cars and trucks were wonderful and well aware of our story and top speed situation. Of course, whenever possible and safe to do so, we would pull off the road and allow them to pass.

Probably the most asked question of us was: "How are you coping living in such close quarters with your siblings?" To us this was a very unusual question, because we all get on so well and always will. There were never any problems with each other only with vehicles or other surroundings. This trip that started out as a road trip for Steve became the trip of a lifetime for all of us, something we will never forget.

Parked outside the house next door to the motel that now stands where Charlie's house was located on the Melbourne Road in Geelong.

Heard family Acknowledgments

As with all great stories and adventures like this, there are special people that need to be acknowledged, whether for sponsorship or just plain good friendship. I'm sure these people won't want special mention, but I am going to anyway. They are not in any particular order.

Gavin Stuart, Yellow Express Taxi Trucks

Dick Smith Foods – Lynda Hayes

Billy Thompson – Thompson Transport

Spencer and Wendy Yarrow

Duncan from Top Cogg and Penrite Oils

Peter Eaton – Clare, South Australia

Our wives and families

Scott Greasham, our "adopted brother"

Simon Purssey – 13 CABS (now a lifelong friend)

Publisher's Acknowledgments

In researching this book I have used many sources, often to corroborate or to add extra details to events, places or background of people mentioned in the basic story. This information came from many sources and was sometimes obtained from more than one source. Therefore I would like to acknowledge as many of those sources as possible, but in particular the following:

The Heard Family for oral history and Scott Greasham for colour photographs.

The staff at Alice Springs Library for access to their vast resources of information relating to Central Australia contained in their "Alice Springs Collection".

National Road Transport Hall of Fame Alice Springs from which many details of early inland travel were garnered and/or verified.

Publications

Explorations in Australia - John McDouall Stuart (1865) facsimile edition 1984, Hesperian Press, Carlisle WA 6101.

Exploring the Stuart Highway & The Oodnadatta Track (6th Edition), Tourist Information Distributors Australia, Balhannah SA 5242.

Telegraph Stations of Central Australia - Historical Photographs, NT Print Management, Alice Springs.

Flynn of the Inland - Ion L. Idriess, Angus and Robertson (1932) Reprinted edition 1955.

The Territory - Ernestine Hill, Angus and Robertson (1951) Reprinted edition 1955.

Lasseter's Last Ride - Ion Idriess, Angus and Robertson (1931) Reprinted edition 1952.

Central Australia - CT Madigan, Oxford University Press New revised edition 1944.

Crossing the Dead Heart - CT Madigan, Rigby Limited (1946) Reprinted edition 1974.

The Alice - The Story of Alice Springs - Alice Springs Branch of the Country Women's Association 1960.

Mr Stuart's Track - The Forgotten Life of Australia's Greatest Explorer - John Bailey, MACMILLAN 2006.

Nature's Pilgrim - Life Journeys of Captain S.A. White, Naturalist - Rob Linn 1989, Historical Consultants.

Alice On The Line - Doris Blackwell, Douglas Lockwood, Outback Books/New Holland Publishers (Australia) Pty Ltd (1965) Reprinted edition 2001.

Australia's Northern Secret - Tourism in the Northern Territory, 1920s to 1980s - Baiba Berzins 2007

The Shackle - DE Kelsey/Ira Nesdale, Lynton Publications Pty Ltd, Blackwood SA 5051 1975.

Telegraph Tourists - Crossing Australia with "Vauxie" and "Baby" in 1929 - Frank Wright & Penryn Goldman, Jimaringle Publications 1993, Mount Martha Vic. 3934.

The Man From Oodnadatta - RB Plowman, Angus and Robertson (1933) Third edition 1957.

Australia's Muslim Cameleers - Pioneers of the Inland 1860s-1930s - Philip Jones and Anna Kenny, Wakefield Press, Kent Town SA 5067.

The Herald Road Guide 1930 Motor Roads of Victoria, and routes to Sydney and Adelaide in Speedo Maps, Edgar H Baillie, Herald and Weekly Times Limited, Melbourne.

The Courier-Mail Motor Road Guide - Published by arrangement with the Royal Automobile Club of Queensland 1934.